THE CAN(
OF T...
ROMAN CATHOLIC CHURCH
AND THE
CHURCH OF ENGLAND

THE CANON LAW
OF THE
ROMAN CATHOLIC CHURCH
AND THE
CHURCH OF ENGLAND

≈

A Handbook

≈

RHIDIAN JONES

T&T CLARK
EDINBURGH

T&T CLARK LTD
59 GEORGE STREET
EDINBURGH EH2 2LQ
SCOTLAND
www.tandtclark.co.uk

First published 2000

ISBN 0 567 08717 4

British Library Cataloguing-in-Publication Data
A catalogue record for this book is available from the British Library

\

Typeset by Waverley Typesetters, Galashiels
Printed and bound in Great Britain by MPG Books, Bodmin

Contents

Contents

Preface

The aim of this dictionary is to provide easy reference and quick accessibility to the current canon law of the Roman Catholic Church and the Church of England. I hope that it will prove useful and stimulating not only for scholars and clerics engaged in the exercise of canon law, but also for all with an interest in Church law.

When an article headword is directly derived from Greek or Latin, the Latin or Greek term is given in parentheses, together with a translation where necessary. A few terms are of historical interest, e.g. 'Decretals', 'Queen Anne's Bounty'. Some common terms found in Eastern Catholic Churches, e.g. 'eparchy', 'exarchy', are also included. Cross-references to other entries are distinguished typographically, as are words which appear elsewhere as entries. The Appendices at the end of the book contain changes in the Universal Law of the Roman Catholic Church which are outside the 1983 code of canon law.

Where a particular Church shows no vestige of a parallel institution (formal or informal) to the discussed institution, no entry is made for that Church.

Certain words found in Anglican jurisprudence which have no equivalent in the Church of England are included (e.g. 'Panchayat', 'Code', 'Ecumenical Concordats'), as are Roman Catholic terms employed in the wider Anglican Communion but not in the Church of England (e.g. 'co-adjutor bishop', 'auxiliary bishop'). I hope that this will give the dictionary a wider appeal – beyond the Church of England, and to members of other Anglican Churches within the worldwide Communion.

Although the congregations of the Roman *Curia* are no longer styled 'sacred', I have included this adjective when citing those bodies that were so called before 1983.

I owe an enormous debt of gratitude to Dr Norman Doe of the Cardiff Law School for encouraging me to study for the Cardiff LLM in canon law, and to embark upon this work; also for his unstinting support and boundless enthusiasm. A special debt is due to Father Robert Ombres OP of Blackfriars, Oxford, for his gentle and helpful advice at all times. Without their kindness and keen scholarship this venture would have been impossible. I would like to record my gratitude to the Rt Revd John McAreavey, Bishop of Dromore, formerly Professor of Canon Law at St Patrick's

College, Maynooth, for his help and hospitality during my research at the college. I am also grateful to Dr Hanns Engelhardt, and to Mr Brian Hanson CBE, Registrar of the Provinces of Canterbury and York, for their warm interest, information and advice; to Paul Barber of the Catholic Education Service for updating me on current developments in Roman Catholic canon law; also to Dr Roma Bhattacharjea, Dr Marianne Dorman, Father Richard Duffield CO, Dr Tamara Grdzelidze, Samantha Rhydderch and Michael Rowett. Finally, I would like to thank Cathy Brocklehurst and Carol Jordan for their suggestions, patience and thoroughness in typing the script.

RHIDIAN JONES
The St Theosevia Centre for Christian Spirituality
Oxford

Abbreviations

AAS	*Acta Apostolicae Sedis*
ABA	Appointment of Bishops Act, 1533
AC	The Anglican Communion
ACC	Anglican Consultative Council
AG	Attorney-General
art(s).	article(s)
AS	Anglo-Saxon
ASB	Alternative Service Book (1980)
BCP	Book of Common Prayer (1662)
CA	Court of Appeal
can.	canon
C(A and R)M	Churchwardens (Appointment and Resignation) Measure, 1964
canon	A canon ecclesiastical promulgated by the Convocations of Canterbury and York in 1964 and 1969, and by the General Synod of the Church of England from 1970
CC	Congregation for the Clergy
c(cc)	canon(s) in the 1983 *Codex Iuris Canonici*
CCEJM	Care of Churches and Ecclesiastical Jurisdiction Measure, 1991
CCEO	*Codex Canonum Ecclesiarum Orientalium* (Vatican Press, 1990: the Eastern Catholic code of canon law)
CC(SP)M	Care of Cathedrals (Supplementary Provisions) Measure, 1994
CD	Vatican II Decree *Christus Dominus* (1965)
Ch	Chancellor

CIC	*Codex Iuris Canonici* (Libreria Editrice Vaticana, 1983: the Roman Catholic code of canon law)
CLD	*Canon Law Digest*
C of E	Church of England
C of E A(P)A	Church of England Assembly (Powers) Act, 1919
C of E (MP)M	Church of England (Miscellaneous Provisions) Measures, 1976 and 1992
C of E (W and D)M	Church of England (Worship and Doctrine) Measure, 1974
CM	Cathedrals Measure, 1963
Const.	Constitution
corr.	corrupted
CRR	Church Representation Rules (schedule 3 to the Synodical Government Measure, 1969)
CWIS	Common Worship: Initiation Services (1998)
CYCLC	The Christian Year: Calendar, Lectionary and Collects (1997)
DM	Dioceses Measure, 1978
EC	Eastern Catholic Churches
eccl.	ecclesiastical
ECUSA	Protestant Episcopal Church in the United States of America
EDM	Ecclesiastical Delapidations Measure, 1923
E. Ind.	East Indian
EJM	Ecclesiastical Jurisdiction Measure, 1963
ELJ	*Ecclesiastical Law Journal*
EMAS	Episcopal Ministry Act of Synod, 1993
F	French
FJM	Faculty Jurisdiction Measure, 1964
FJR	Faculty Jurisdiction Rules, 1992
Gk	Greek
GS	General Synod (of the Church of England)
GS	Vatican II pastoral constitution *Gaudium et Spes* (1965)
HL	House of Lords

HLE	Halsbury, *Laws of England*, vol. 14: *Ecclesiastical Law* (4th edn., London, 1975)
in re	concerning
instr.	instrument
intr.	introduction
I(VB)M	Incumbents (Vacation of Benefices) Measure, 1977 (as amended in 1993)
J	Judge (Mr Justice)
L	Latin
LC	Lambeth Conference
leg.	legal
LG	Vatican II dogmatic constitution *Lumen Gentium* (1964)
lit.	literally
lit. circ.	circular letter
MA	Marriage Act, 1949 and 1983
MCA	Matrimonial Causes Act, 1965
ME	*Monitor Ecclesiasticus* (Rome, 1948–)
MIECL	T. Briden and B. Hanson, eds., *Moore's Introduction to English Canon Law* (3rd edn., 1992)
OC	The Orthodox Church
OF	Old French
OUI	Sacred Congregation for Divine Worship: *Ordo Unctionis Infirmorum Eorumque Pastoralis Curae* (1972)
PA	Pluralities Act, 1838
PB	John Paul II: apostolic constitution *Pastor Bonus* (1988)
P(B)M	Patronage (Benefices) Measure, 1986
PCC	Parochial Church Council
PCC(P)M	Parochial Church Council (Powers) Measure, 1956
per	through, by
PM	Pastoral Measure, 1983
P(OW)M	Priests (Ordination of Women) Measure, 1993

PRRM	Parochial Registers and Records Measure, 1978 (as amended by the Church of England (Miscellaneous Provisions) Measure, 1992)
r.(rr.)	rules
RC	Roman Catholic Church
res(s).	resolution(s)
s.(ss.)	section(s)
SA	Simony Act, 1588
SBA	Suffragan Bishops Act, 1534
SC	Vatican II constitution on the Sacred Liturgy *Sacrosanctum Concilium* (1963)
SCA	Submission of the Clergy Act 1533
SCC	Sacred Congregation for the Clergy
SCDF	Sacred Congregation for the Doctrine of the Faith
SCDW	Sacred Congregation for Divine Worship
sched.	schedule
SCHO	Sacred Congregation of the Holy Office
SCRit	Sacred Congregation of Rites
SCRSI	Sacred Congregation for Religious and Secular Institutes
SCSac	Sacred Congregation of the Discipline of Sacraments
SGM	Synodical Government Measure, 1969
SMC	John Paul II: apostolic constitution *Spirituali Militum Curae* (1986)
UDG	John Paul II: apostolic constitution *Universi Dominici Gregis* (1996)
Vatican II	The Second Vatican Council (1962–5)
VP	Paul VI: apostolic constitution *Vicariae Potestatis* (1977)

Doctrinal Documents of the Roman Catholic Church

Papal Documents

Pius XI
Encyclical letter *Casti Conubii* (1930)
Encyclical letter *Quadragesimo Anno* (1931)

Pius XII
Allocution to the Rota (1942)
Allocution to midwives (1957)

Paul VI
Apostolic letter *Ecclesiae Sanctae* (1966)
Apostolic constitution *Indulgentiarum Doctrina* (1967)
Apostolic letter *Ministeria Quaedam* (1972)
Encyclical letter *Humanae Vitae* (1968)
Apostolic constitution *Vicariae Potestatis* (1977)

John Paul II
Apostolic constitutions:
    Divinus Perfectionis Magister (1983)
    Sacrae Disciplinae Leges (1983)
    Spirituali Militum Curae (1986)
    Pastor Bonus (1988)
    Universi Dominici Gregis (1996)

Apostolic exhortations:
    Familiaris Consortio (1981)
    Christifideles Laici (1988)

Apostolic letters:
    Duodecimum Saeculum (1987)
    Ad Tuendam Fidem (1998)

Encyclical letters:
    Redemptor Hominis (1979)
    Slavorum Apostoli (1985)
    Veritatis Splendor (1993)

Letter to Cardinal Ratzinger, Prefect of the Congregation for the Doctrine of the Faith (1988)

Message to the People of Asia (1981)

Roman Curial Documents

SCC instruction *Sollemne Semper* (1957)

SCDF declaration *De Abortu Procurato* (1974)

CDF instruction *Donum Vitae* (1987)

SCDW directory *Pueros Baptizatos* (1973)

SCDW instruction on the Roman Missal (1970)

SCDW *Ordo Infirmorum Eorumque Pastoralis Curae* (1972)

SCHO instruction *Piam et Constantem* (1963)

SCRit instruction *Eucharisticum Mysterium* (1967)

SCRSI instruction *Venite Seorsum* (1969)

CSac circular letter *De processu super matrimonio rato et non consummato* (1986)

Vatican II Documents

Constitution on the Sacred Liturgy *Sacrosanctum Concilium* (1963)

Dogmatic constitution *Lumen Gentium* (1964)

Decree on ecumenism *Unitatis Redintegratio* (1964)

Decree *Christus Dominus* (1965)

Declaration *Dignitatis Humanae* (1965)

Decree *Perfectae Caritatis* (1965)

Pastoral constitution *Gaudium et Spes* (1965)

Table of Cases

Table of
Parliamentary Statutes

Abortion Act, 1967

Act of Supremacy, 1558

Appointment of Bishops Act, 1533

Church of England Assembly (Powers) Act, 1919

City of London (Guild Churches) Act, 1952

Compulsory Church Rate Abolition Act, 1868

Ecclesiastical Commissioners Acts, 1836 and 1850

Education Reform Act, 1988

Infant Life (Preservation) Act, 1929

Marriage Act, 1949

Matrimonial Causes Act, 1965

Pluralities Act, 1838

Queen Anne's Bounty Act, 1703

Simony Act, 1588

Submission of the Clergy Act, 1533

Suffragan Bishops Act, 1534

Tithes and Offerings Act, 1548

Table of Measures
of the Church of England

Care of Cathedrals (Supplementary Provisions) Measure, 1994

Care of Churches and Ecclesiastical Jurisdiction Measure, 1991

Cathedrals Measure, 1963

Church Commissioners Measure, 1947

Church of England (Miscellaneous Provisions) Measures, 1976, 1992

Church of England (Worship and Doctrine) Measure, 1974

Churchwardens (Appointment and Resignation) Measure, 1964

Dioceses Measure, 1978

Ecclesiastical Delapidations Measure, 1923

Ecclesiastical Jurisdiction Measure, 1963

Endowments and Glebe Measure, 1976

Extra-Parochial Ministry Measure, 1967

Faculty Jurisdiction Measure, 1964

First Fruits and Tenths Measure, 1926

Incumbents (Vacation of Benefices) Measures, 1977 and 1993

Inspection of Churches Measure, 1955

Parochial Church Council (Powers) Measure, 1956

Parochial Registers and Records Measure, 1978

Pastoral Measure, 1983

Patronage (Benefices) Measure, 1986

Priests (Ordination of Women) Measure, 1993

Synodical Government Measure, 1969

Church of England Rules

Church of England Reports, Resolutions, Statements and Guidelines

A

ABBOT (L *abbas*)

RC. The moderator of an abbey, i.e. an autonomous monastery. The abbot is judge of first INSTANCE if there is a controversy between the religious of an autonomous monastery (c 1427 §1). **Abbot Superior**: the superior of a monastic congregation (c 620). He is judge of first instance where there is contention between two monasteries (c 1427 §2). **Abbot Primate**: the abbot who governs a certain monastic congregation established within a territorial boundary forming a territorial abbacy. He functions like a diocesan BISHOP (c 370).

C of E. The superior of a Benedictine religious community. Like all superiors of religious communities he has 'responsibility for the common good and good of each member' and he 'exercises a ministry of oversight and service towards the community' (see *Directory of the Religious Life* (4th edn., London, 1990), para. 908).

ABJURATION (L *abjuratio*)

RC. The process by which apostates, heretics and schismatics renounce their errors in order to be reconciled to the Church. See **Apostasy**; **Heresy**; **Schism**.

ABORTION (L *abortus*)

RC. The taking of the life of the foetus in the mother's womb. The CANON LAW and teaching of the Church prohibit abortion. The taking of the life of offspring in the womb is not justified on any ground; it is a grave crime (Pius XI: encyclical letter *Casti Connubii* (1930)). 'It is an act which is hostile to life itself' (*GS* 27; John Paul II: encyclical letter *Veritatis Splendor* (1993), 80(1)). It is not allowed even for therapeutic reasons (Paul VI: encyclical letter *Humanae Vitae* (1968), 14). It is a violation of the right to life (SCDF declaration *De Abortu Procurato* (1974), 12). Human life is inviolable from the moment of conception (CDF instruction *Donum Vitae* (1987), Intr. 4). All who are directly involved in procuring an abortion incur a LATAE SENTENTIAE EXCOMMUNICATION (c 1398) and are forbidden from receiving holy ORDERS (c 1041) and from exercising them (c 1044 §1).

C of E. The Church opposes 'any form of victimisation or discrimination against surgeons, doctors, nurses and medical, health or social workers who cannot, in conscience, assist in or recommend abortion' (General

Synod Resolution, July 1975; *Abortion and the Church: A Report by the Board for Social Responsibility* (London, 1993). A foetus which is 'capable of being born alive' (i.e. of living and breathing through its own lungs) is a child (Infant Life (Preservation) Act 1929 s. 1; also *Rance* v. *Mid-Downs Health Authority* [1991] 1 All ER 801). According to s. 4(1) of the Abortion Act, 1967 'no person shall be under any duty, whether by contract or by statutory or other legal requirement, to participate in any treatment authorised by this Act to which he has a conscientious objection'. It has been held that a refusal by a medical secretary on conscientious grounds to type a letter of referral for an abortion does not amount to 'participation' within the meaning of the Act (*Janway* v. *Salford Health Authority* [1988] 3 All ER 1079). The whole process of medical induction has to be carried out by a doctor and not merely under a doctor's instructions, in order to come within the Act (*Royal College of Nursing* v. *DHSS* [1981] 1 All ER 545).

ABROGATION (L *abrogatio*)

RC. The repeal of a law (see c 6); UNIVERSAL and PARTICULAR LAWS which are not contrary to *CIC* are not abrogated, nor are particular NORMS contrary to it if it grants them EXCEPTION. See **Derogation**.

ABSOLUTION (L *absolutio*)

RC. The priestly ministry of imparting God's forgiveness of sins upon those who are penitent (c 959). **Collective** or **general absolution**: absolution imparted to a number of penitents at the same time without previous individual CONFESSION when they are in danger of death or a grave necessity exists (c 961 §1). The diocesan BISHOP judges whether a grave necessity exists by employing criteria agreed upon by the conference of bishops (c 961 §2). For a penitent to 'benefit validly' from absolution given to a number of penitents at the same time, he or she has to resolve to confess in 'due time' each GRAVE SIN involved (c 962 §1). A person who has received the remission of serious sins by a general absolution is required to make an individual confession before receiving another general absolution (c 963).

C of E. The absolving of sins by a bishop or PRIEST in the name and power of Christ. Absolution can be given generally and publicly in a CHURCH service, or individually and privately after confession to God in the presence of a priest. No priest is allowed to exercise the ministry of absolution in any place without the permission of the minister having the cure of souls (except where a person is in danger of death or there is urgent cause: canon B29(4)). See canon B29.

ACEPHALUS (L *acephalus*, Gk ἀκέφαλος)

RC. A CLERIC who is not incardinated in any way but is itinerant. See **Incardination**; *Peregrinus*; *Vagus*.

ACOLYTE (L *acolythus*)

RC. An EXTRAORDINARY MINISTER of Holy Communion whose ministry includes serving at Mass and distributing the EUCHARIST (c 910). Lay men can be installed to this ministry subject to the conditions stated in c 230 (see Paul VI: *Ministeria Quaedam* (1972)). See **Lector**.

C of E. There may be an equivalent ministry, but there is no formal law on the subject.

ACT (L *actus*)

RC. An act. A **juridic act**: a manifest act of will intended to have a juridic effect (e.g. the conferral of and removal from office: see cc 124–8). An **administrative act**: an act or ordinance issued by a public authority having the power of JURISDICTION which acts in an administrative capacity. A *singular or particular administrative act*: an act (e.g. DECREE, PRECEPT, RESCRIPT, DISPENSATION or privilege) directed at an individual (cc 35–93). An *extraordinary administrative act*: the administration of ecclesiastical goods belonging to a public JURIDICAL PERSON in a DIOCESE for the sake of economic stability; such an act is the responsibility of the ORDINARY who is obliged to consult with the Finance Council and the College of Consultors in order to obtain their approval; such an act is defined by the conference of BISHOPS (c 1277).

C of E. Legislation in the form of a statute enacted by the Sovereign in Parliament which may have direct or indirect applicability to the established Church, e.g. C of E A(P)A, 1919 and Education Reform Act, 1988. **Act of Convocation**: a resolution passed by the Houses of the CONVOCATIONS OF CANTERBURY AND YORK. Such a resolution has been judicially held to have moral but no legal force (*Bland* v. *Archdeacon of Cheltenham* [1972] 1 All ER 1012 at 1018). **Act of Synod** ('Episcopal Ministry Act of Synod'): an Act passed by the GENERAL SYNOD to provide alternative episcopal oversight for PARISHES opposed to the ORDINATION and ministry of women as PRIESTS, and for related matters. It is a form of regulatory instrument having only moral force. See **Provincial Episcopal Visitor**.

ACTA (L *actus*)

RC. Documents. **Judicial Acts**: documents or materials concerning proofs, sentencing or procedure. Where a person is to be admitted for trial both the acts of the case and the acts of PROCESS (pertaining to procedure) are to be put in writing (c 1472). *Acta Apostolicae Sedis*:

the official gazette or register of the Apostolic See containing the Universal Laws of the Church. These laws usually become effective three months after their publication in the register.

Act *inter Vivos* (L, between the living)

RC. A legal arrangement made by a person during his or her lifetime to transfer property to a particular person or corporate body, which takes effect forthwith (cc 1299 §1; 1300–2. See **Act *Mortis Causa*.**

Actio de Spolio (L, lawsuit over deprivations)

RC. A suit to recover property of which one has been deprived. The plaintiff is free to file his petition with the tribunal of the disputed object or with one of the other tribunals of the ordinary Forum (cc 1407 §1; 1410).

Act *Mortis Causa* (L, because of death).

RC. A legal arrangement made by a person during his or her lifetime to transfer property to a particular person or corporate body, which takes effect only after death (cc 1299 §§1, 2; 1300–2. See **Act *inter Vivos*.**

Ad limina visit (L, to the thresholds)

RC. A visit to the Apostolic See which a diocesan Bishop is bound to make every five years in order to present the pope with a report concerning the state of his Diocese. Such a visit is to include a pilgrimage to the tombs of St Peter and St Paul, a personal meeting with the pope and meetings with the Dicasteries of the Roman Curia (*PB* art. 31). A report on the state of a diocese is to be forwarded to the Apostolic See six months before a visit (*PB* art. 32). During the visit the pope 'confirms and supports' his brother bishops in faith and charity. The visit 'strengthens the bonds of hierarchical communion and openly manifests the catholicity of the Church and the unity of the episcopal college' (*PB* art. 29). See **Appendix III**; cc 399–400.

Administrator (L)

RC. A Cleric or lay person who through a legitimate title takes part in the administration of ecclesiastical goods (c 1282; also cc 1283, 1284, 1289). **Apostolic administrator**: see **Apostolic Administration**. **Diocesan administrator**: a Priest or Bishop who is elected by the College of Consultors to govern a vacant See. He is bound by the obligations and enjoys the power of the diocesan bishop (cc 427 §1; 416–38). **Parochial administrator**: a priest appointed by the diocesan bishop who substitutes for the pastor when a PARISH becomes vacant or when the pastor is prevented from exercising his pastoral office by reason of ill health, imprisonment, exile, etc. (cc 539–40). See **Lay Worker**; *Sede Vacante*; **Vicar**.

ADOPTION (L *adoptio*)

RC. Children adopted according to civil law NORMS are considered as being the children of the person or persons who have adopted them (c 110). An adoptive parent is prevented by an ecclesiastical IMPEDIMENT from contracting a valid MARRIAGE with his or her adopted child. This impediment also invalidates a marriage between an adopted brother or sister (c 1094). See **Affinity**; **Consanguinity**.

ADORATION OF THE EUCHARIST (L *adoratio Eucharistiae*)

RC. Adoration of the blessed EUCHARIST (or blessed SACRAMENT, as it is also called) outside Mass is encouraged. CHURCHES where the blessed Eucharist is reserved are to be kept open for a period every day to enable the faithful to pray before the blessed Sacrament (c 937). Exposition of the blessed Sacrament in a ciborium or a monstrance is permitted, and also Eucharistic benediction. This practice 'stimulates the faithful to an awareness of the marvellous presence of Christ, and is an invitation to spiritual communion with him' (SCRit: instr. *Eucharisticum Mysterium* (1967), 60; SCDW: *Holy Communion and Worship of the Eucharist outside Mass*, 82–92.

C of E. A BCP RUBRIC forbids adoration of the consecrated elements. Furthermore, articles 25 and 28 of the Thirty-Nine Articles state respectively: 'The Sacraments were not ordained of Christ to be gazed upon, or to be carried about, but that we should duly use them' and 'The Sacrament of the Lord's Supper was not by Christ's ordinance reserved, carried about, lifted up, or worshipped'. These articles, however, are not now enforced.

ADVENA (L, stranger)

RC. A 'newcomer' or temporary resident. A person who lives in his or her place of quasi-DOMICILE (c 100).

ADVOCATE (L *advocatus*)

RC. A person approved by ecclesiastical authority who safeguards the rights of one of the parties in a canonical PROCESS (cc 1481–90). An advocate has to be appointed (either by the accused or by the court) when a penal trial is undertaken (c 1481 §2), and in a contentious trial which involves minors or the public good, except for MARRIAGE cases (c 1481 §3). **Advocates of consistories**: advocates involved with organisations of the Roman CURIA. **Advocates of the Roman Rota, advocates of the Causes for Saints** and **advocates of the Apostolic Signatura** plead before different INSTANCES. See **Rota**.

AFFINITY (L *affinitas*)

RC. A relationship which arises from a valid MARRIAGE and which exists between a man and the blood relatives of the woman, and conversely. Blood relatives of the man are related in the same line (direct or collateral) and degree (the spouses are regarded as a single person) by affinity to the woman and conversely (c 109). The IMPEDIMENT of affinity prohibits marriage between one spouse and any one of the other spouse's relatives in the direct line (e.g. stepchildren: c 1092). Degrees of affinity in the collateral line (i.e. the relationship between one spouse and any relations of the other spouse's relations) are not prohibited. The impediment does not affect marriages of the un-baptized or of baptized non-Catholics. See **Consanguinity**.

C of E. According to canon B31 ('Of Certain Impediments to Marriages') no person is allowed to marry within the prohibited degrees: 'all marriages purported to be made within the said degrees are void'. A table of the prohibited degrees is set out in the canon and also in the BCP.

AGNATION (L *agnatio*)

RC. Blood relationship through the male line, as opposed to COGNATION (which is through the female line). There is no distinction in CANON LAW between the two expressions of CONSANGUINITY. See **Impediment**.

ALIENATION (L *alienatio*)

RC. The transferring of ownership to another party of ecclesiastical property which is part of the 'stable patrimony' of a JURIDICAL PERSON (cc 1291–6). The diocesan BISHOP is to listen to the advice of the finance council and the college of consultors before administering the temporal goods of the DIOCESE (c 1277). Alienation of temporal goods of a value higher than that determined in law (e.g. money, stock, bonds, etc.) requires the permission of a competent authority (e.g. the bishops' conference). A person who alienates ecclesiastical goods without the necessary permission is punishable with a just PENALTY (c 1377). See *Beneplacitum*; *Bona Ecclesiastica*.

ALMS (L *eleemosyna*, Gk ἐλεημοσύνη)

RC. Money given to the Church in charity; an offering. The Christian faithful are obliged to assist with the needs of the Church (c 222 §1).

The Church has an innate right to seek necessary support from the Christian faithful (c 1260). This is so because they share in the mission of the Church. See **Laity**.

C of E. CHURCHWARDENS as agents of the PCC are to collect and dispose of alms and other offerings which are given during the Communion service (canon B17A; also PCC(P)M s. 7(iv)). If the minister and the PCC cannot agree how the alms of the people should be applied, the ORDINARY is to determine their disposal (canon F10).

ALTAR (L *altarium*)

RC. A table on which the Eucharistic Sacrifice is celebrated (cc 1235–9).

C of E. The Lord's Table where the PRIEST says the prayer of consecration over the bread and wine at Holy Communion (BCP; canon F2). It has been judicially determined that since 'a doctrine of the Eucharistic sacrifice which is not that of a repetition of the sacrifice of Calvary can lawfully be held in the Church of England' it is lawful and proper to call the Lord's Table an altar (*Re St Stephen's, Walbrook* [1987] 2 All ER 587 at 58).

AMOTION: see **Removal from Office**.

ANALOGY (L *analogia*)

RC. A judicial or executive DECREE, SENTENCE or decision having full legal standing, which remedies a *lacuna* or gap in a law or CUSTOM by supporting a particular right or redressing a particular injustice. In filling a gap in the law recourse must be made to decisions in analogous cases, jurisprudence, canonical EQUITY and the opinions of learned persons. The doctrine of *lacuna* cannot be extended to matters of penal law (c 19). See **Lacuna Legis**.

ANGLICAN COMMUNION

AC. 'A fellowship, within the One Holy Catholic and Apostolic Church, of those duly constituted Dioceses, Provinces or Regional Churches in communion with the See of Canterbury', upholding the faith and order as they are generally set forth in the BCP as authorized in their several Churches, and 'bound together not by a central legislative and executive authority, but by mutual loyalty sustained through the common counsel of the Bishops in Conference' (LC 1930, ress. 48, 49). The Anglican Communion is composed of thirty-seven self-governing Churches.

ANGLICAN CONSULTATIVE COUNCIL

C of E. A consultative body alongside the LAMBETH CONFERENCE of Anglican BISHOPS, consisting of the Archbishop of Canterbury and three (a bishop, a PRIEST or DEACON and a lay person) or two (a bishop and a priest, deacon or lay person) delegates from each independent PROVINCE of the ANGLICAN COMMUNION. It meets between the Lambeth Conferences. Its functions include advising on inter-Anglican relations and arranging for pan-Anglican conversations with the Roman Catholic Church and the Orthodox Churches.

ANNULMENT OF MARRIAGE: see **Nullity**.

ANOINTING OF THE SICK (L *unctio infirmorum*)

RC. One of the seven SACRAMENTS of the Church. The sacrament can only be validly administered by a PRESBYTER (c 1003 §1). PRIESTS having the care of souls are obliged to administer the sacrament to the seriously ill and infirm who are under their pastoral care (c 1003 §2). Anointing is not to be administered to persons 'who obstinately persist in a manifestly grave sin' (c 1007). The sacrament does not imprint a CHARACTER and may be repeated (c 1004 §2). For the blessing of the oil, see **Oil**; also **Chrism; Chrismation**. See *SC* 73; *OUI* 6; *LG* 11; **Last Rites**.

C of E. The minister is to 'exhort, instruct and comfort' a person who is sick or in danger of death 'in such manner as he shall think most needful and convenient' (canon B37(1)). The priest may anoint such a person if the person 'so desires' (canon B37(3)). See **Oil**.

APOSTASY (L *apostasia*, Gk ἀποστασία)

RC. The total repudiation of the Christian faith by a baptized person (c 751). An apostate from the faith incurs EXCOMMUNICATION *LATAE SENTENTIAE* (c 1364) and is deprived of ecclesiastical funeral rites (as are heretics and schismatics: c 1184). See **Abjuration; Heresy; Schism**.

APOSTOLIC ADMINISTRATION (L *administratio apostolica*)

RC. A certain portion of the people of God governed by an apostolic ADMINISTRATOR, which the pope has not erected into a DIOCESE due to a particular and very serious reason (e.g. where the majority of Christians are non-Catholics c 371 §2). An apostolic administrator can also be appointed to run a vacant SEE (e.g. the Archdiocese of Birmingham in 1999). See **Apostolic Prefecture; Apostolic Vicariate**.

APOSTOLIC CAMERA (L *camera apostolica*)

RC. An administrative office of the Roman *CURIA* which carries out services connected with the pope's household. This historic office looks after the temporal goods of the APOSTOLIC SEE (in particular during a vacancy of the Apostolic See) and is charged with calling together a CONCLAVE (PB171). Its moderator is the CARDINAL CAMERLENGO. See **Conclave**; *Sede Vacante*.

APOSTOLIC DELEGATE (L *delegatus apostolicus*)

RC. A LEGATE of the pope who represents him to a local Church, a conference or an international council (c 363 §2). See **Legate**.

APOSTOLIC LETTER (L *epistula apostolica*)

RC. A letter of the pope. In particular, one which conveys the nomination of a new BISHOP (cc 379, 382). See **Brief**; **Bull**; *Chirographum*; *Motu Proprio*.

APOSTOLIC PREFECTURE (L *praefectura apostolica*)

RC. A territory or portion of the Church not yet erected into a DIOCESE, which is governed by an apostolic prefect in the name of the Supreme Pontiff (c 371). It is a stage in the process whereby a missionary territory becomes a diocese. See **Apostolic Vicariate**.

APOSTOLIC SEE (or **HOLY SEE**) (L *sedes apostolica*, throne of the apostles)

RC. The See of Rome of which the pope is BISHOP. It includes the ROMAN PONTIFF himself and also the Secretariat of State, the Council for the Public Affairs of the Church and other institutions of the Roman CURIA (c 361). See **See**.

APOSTOLIC SIGNATURA (L *signatura apostolica*)

RC. The Apostolic Signatura is the supreme tribunal of the APOSTOLIC SEE. It adjudicates appeals against SENTENCES of the Roman ROTA. Its second section is the supreme administrative tribunal (c 1445).

APOSTOLIC VICARIATE (L *vicariatus apostolica*)

RC. A territory or portion of the Church not yet erected into a DIOCESE, which is governed by an apostolic VICAR in the name of the Supreme Pontiff (c 371). An apostolic vicar, unlike an apostolic prefect, is usually a BISHOP. See **Apostolic Prefecture**.

APPLICATION (L *applicatio*, attaching)

RC. A Mass may be offered ('applied') by a PRIEST for anyone, living or dead (c 901). An offering may lawfully be made to a priest who celebrates Mass in order to apply the Mass according to a definite intention (c 945). See **Eucharist**.

ARBITRATION (L *arbitratus*)

RC. A special procedure between parties for avoiding a trial. A settlement, compromise or a trial by arbiters may be employed (cc 1713–16). See **Transactio**.

ARCHBISHOP (L *archiepiscopus*, Gk ἀρχιεπίσκοπος)

RC. The BISHOP of a metropolitan DIOCESE, or ARCHDIOCESE, who presides over an ecclesiastical PROVINCE (c 435). Not all archbishops are metropolitans.

C of E. The archbishops of Canterbury and York are appointed by the Crown. Each possesses metropolitical JURISDICTION throughout his province. The archbishop's rights and duties include confirming the ELECTION of bishops in his province and presiding as chief consecrator at their CONSECRATION, hearing appeals in his PROVINCIAL COURT, holding metropolitical VISITATIONS, presiding in CONVOCATION and along with his brother archbishop being joint president of the GENERAL SYNOD. The granting of LICENCES and DISPENSATIONS throughout England vests in the Archbishop of Canterbury (canon C17). See also **Diocese**; **Licence**.

ARCHDEACON (L *archidiaconus*, Gk ἀρχιδιάκονος)

RC. There is no equivalent office. See Judicial **Vicar**.

C of E. A PRIEST appointed by the diocesan BISHOP to assist him in his pastoral care and office within an archdeaconry (canon C22(4)); the archdeacon's JURISDICTION is an ORDINARY jurisdiction. He or she also exercises administrative, disciplinary and quasi-judicial functions; they include surveying Church property, carrying out duties under the Inspection of Churches Measure, 1955, inducting priests and holding annual VISITATIONS to examine and maintain Church governance and discipline (canon C22(5)). An archdeacon has a specific function in relation to the FACULTY jurisdiction (CCEJM ss 12, 13, 16, 19, 20; FJR rr. 6, 7, 8). See **Faculty**; **Ordinary**; **Visitation**.

ARCHDIOCESE (L *archidioecesis*, Gk ἀρχιδιοίκησις)

RC. A DIOCESE forming part of an ecclesiastical PROVINCE whose BISHOP is a metropolitan bishop having a special role within the province (c 1439 §1). See **Bishop**; **Diocese**; **See**.

ARCHIEPISCOPAL CHURCH (L *ecclesia archiepiscopalis*)

EC. An entire Eastern Church *SUI IURIS* not endowed with the patriarchal title, which is presided over by a MAJOR ARCHBISHOP who is the metropolitan of a SEE determined or recognized by the Church's supreme authority (*CCEO* c 151). See **Bishop**; **Major Archbishop**.

ARCHPRIEST (L *archipresbyter*, Gk ἀρχιπρεσβύτερος, chief presbyter)
RC. A PRIEST who is placed over a vicariate forane. He is also called a VICAR forane (c 553 §1).

ASSESSOR (L)
RC. One who serves as a consultor to a single judge in a trial. The judge may use two assessors, who may be CLERICS or laypersons of upright life (c 1424). **C of E.** Assessors form the 'jury' in CONSISTORY COURT clergy discipline cases.

ASSOCIATION OF THE FAITHFUL (L *consociatio fidelium*)
RC. A group of the faithful which is open to both men and women, lay and CLERIC. It is distinct from INSTITUTES OF CONSECRATED LIFE and SOCIETIES OF APOSTOLIC LIFE; such a group can be private or public in nature. A **private association**: an association based upon a common covenant agreed by members of the Christian faithful and which is not established by a competent ecclesiastical authority; its aims include perfection of life, public worship and apostolic work (cc 299, 321–6). A **public association**: an association of the Christian faithful established by a competent ecclesiastical authority with the aim of teaching Christian DOCTRINE, promoting public worship, etc. (cc 301, 312–20).

AUDITOR (L, hearer)
RC. One who instructs a judge on a particular case by collecting and presenting all the evidence. The auditor, who may be a CLERIC or a lay person, is designated by a judge or the president of a collegiate tribunal, and approved by the BISHOP (c 1428). Judges of the Roman ROTA are called auditors. **C of E.** A judge of the Chancery Court of York. See **Dean of the Arches**.

AUMBRY
RC. A small recess in the wall of the sanctuary of a CHURCH for keeping books and sacred vessels. It may be used for the purpose of housing the blessed SACRAMENT.
C of E. An aumbry is considered a legal object for the purpose of RESERVATION OF THE EUCHARIST (*Re St Nicholas, Plumstead* [1961] 1 WLR 916). A TABERNACLE, however, is considered an illegal object for such a purpose (*Re Lapford (Devon) Parish Church* [1954] 3 All ER 484).

AUTHENTIC INTERPRETATION (L *interpretatio authentica*, correct interpretation)

   RC. An interpretation of the law which is binding and which is entrusted to the legislator (e.g. the pope or a diocesan BISHOP) or someone to whom the legislator has entrusted this power (c 16). For example, the Pontifical Council for the Interpretation of Legislative Texts is entrusted with the authority to publish interpretations of the Church's UNIVERSAL LAWS which have been approved by pontifical authority (*PB* 155).

B

BANNS (L *bannus*)

RC. A notice of a forthcoming MARRIAGE. The publication of banns was made a requirement for a regular marriage by a DECREE of the Fourth Lateran Council (1215). Banns are a means of enquiry to uncover IMPEDIMENTS to a marriage and to protect pastoral requirements (c 1067). The ORDINARY is obliged to ensure that an investigation is carried out by the pastor according to guidelines laid down by the BISHOPS' conference. The publication of banns can be dispensed with on pastoral grounds (c 85).

C of E. Since Lord Hardwicke's Marriage Act (1753) a marriage without banns has been invalid in law. Banns have to be published on three Sundays before a marriage (MA s. 7(1)). If a marriage is not solemnized within three months of the publication of banns the publication is void (ibid. s. 12(2)). A marriage may be solemnized after the publication of banns, or 'on the authority of a special licence' or 'on the authority of a "common licence"', or 'on the authority of a certificate issued by a superintendent registrar' (canon B34).

BAPTISM (L *baptisma*, Gk βάπτισμα)

RC. A SACRAMENT which is necessary for salvation, and 'the gateway to the sacraments'. A valid baptism requires the use of pure water and a certain form of words ('I baptize you in the name of the Father, and of the Son, and of the Holy Spirit'). 'By it people are freed from sins, are born again as children of God and made like to Christ by an indelible character, are incorporated into the Church' (c 849). It is the first of the three sacraments required for full Christian initi-ation (baptism, CONFIRMATION and the EUCHARIST) (c 842 §2). Baptism is normally administered by a BISHOP, a PRIEST or a DEACON (c 861 §1). Proper preparation is required: an adult seeking baptism is to be admitted to the catechumenate and, as far as possible, brought through the various stages to sacramental initiation (c 851, 1°); parents and sponsors of an infant who is to be baptized are to be suitably instructed (c 851, 2°). Public baptism is encouraged: baptism is recommended on Sundays or at the Easter Vigil (c 856). **Conditional baptism**: if there is doubt over whether a person was baptized or whether the sacrament was conferred validly, the person is to be baptized conditionally (c 869 §1). In cases of NECESSITY baptism may be conferred in private houses or in hospitals, with the permission of the ORDINARY (c 860 §§1, 2). See **Catechumen**.

C of E. One of the two sacraments (the other being the Eucharist) which are necessary for salvation (BCP). It is validly administered with the use of pure water and with the invocation of the Father, of the Son, and of the Holy Ghost (BCP; ASB; CWIS; *Kemp* v. *Wickes* (1809) 3 Phill at 269). Baptism is normally administered by an ordained minister who has the cure of souls (canon B21); however, baptism by a lay person is valid (*Kemp* v. *Wickes*). The minister has a duty to instruct, or cause to be instructed, a candidate for adult baptism (canon B24(1)); BCP; ASB; CWIS. He or she has a duty in cases of infant baptism to instruct 'the parents or guardians of an infant to be admitted to Holy Baptism that the same responsibilities rest on them as are in the service of Holy Baptism required of the godparents' (canon B22(3)). The effect of baptism is 'a death unto sin, and a new birth unto righteousness' (BCP; ASB; CWIS). The baptized is made a child of God by adoption and incorporated into the Church (BCP). **Conditional baptism**: This is provided for canonically. When the validity of a former baptism is held in question, the person 'desiring to be received into the Church of England . . . shall be instructed and conditionally baptized' (canon B28(1)). Also, when there is doubt concerning the baptism of a candidate for confirmation, the minister is to conditionally baptize him or her (canon B27(5)). Provision is made for baptism in private houses, hospitals, nursing homes, etc. in situations of 'grave cause and necessity' (canon B22(7), (9)). In extreme cases 'No minister being informed of the weakness or danger of death of any infant within his cure and therefore desired to go to baptize the same shall either refuse or delay to do so' (canon B22(6)).

BEATIFICATION (L *beatificatio*)

RC. The act by which the Supreme Pontiff permits the public veneration of a faithful departed Catholic. Permission is usually granted for the veneration of the person beatified in a particular part of the Church (e.g. a particular country or a religious ORDER) rather than throughout the whole Church. The beatified person is given the title of 'Blessed', e.g. Blessed Dominic Barberi (who is venerated in England and Wales). See **Beatification**; **Canonization**; **Venerable**; **Appendix I**.

BENEFICE (L *beneficium*)

RC. An office which carries with it the right to income from the emoluments attached to it. The system of benefice has almost disappeared under *CIC*, which lays greater emphasis on the importance of ecclesiastical office than on the revenues which flow from it. Where benefices still exist, their emoluments and incomes are gathered into a central diocesan institute for the support of the clergy of the DIOCESE (cc 1272, 1274).

C of E. A FREEHOLD office held by an INCUMBENT, who may also be known as the RECTOR or VICAR. He or she has a freehold interest in the emoluments of the benefice (i.e. income from the land or the tithes) during office. The incumbent also has the cure of souls within the PARISH (PM s. 86). A team rector also holds a benefice, but not usually as a freehold but rather as a term of years (PM s. 20(2)). 'Benefice' is defined as 'the office of rector or vicar of a parish or parishes, with cure of souls, but not including the office of vicar in a team ministry or any office in a Cathedral Church' (P(B)M s. 39(1); see also I(VB)M s. 19). See **Patronage**.

BENEPLACITUM (L, good pleasure)

RC. Authority or consent for certain ACTS given by a superior authority, e.g. the consent of the HOLY SEE for the ALIENATION of ecclesiastical goods. See **Alienation**; *Bona Ecclesiastica*.

BINATION (AND TRINATION) (L *binatio*, duplication, bination)

RC. The celebration by a PRIEST of two or three Masses on the same day. Priests are forbidden to celebrate or concelebrate the EUCHARIST more than once a day except when the law permits it (c 905 §1); the law permits priests to celebrate three Masses at Christmas and two at Easter. The local ORDINARY may permit priests to celebrate twice or three times on Sundays and FEASTS OF OBLIGATION when there is pastoral need (c 905 §2).

BISHOP (L *episcopus*, Gk ἐπίσκοπος)

RC. A CLERIC who belongs to the sacred ORDER of bishops. A bishop is a pastor in the Church, a teacher of DOCTRINE, a PRIEST of sacred worship and a minister of governance (cc 375–80). It is the APOSTOLIC SEE who finally decides upon the suitability of a candidate for episcopal office (c 378 §2). **Diocesan bishop**: a bishop with the care of a DIOCESE (c 376). **Titular bishop**: a bishop without the care of a diocese (c 376). **Auxiliary bishop**: a bishop with special FACULTIES appointed to assist the diocesan bishop; he does not possess the right of succession (c 403 §§1, 2). **Coadjutor bishop**: a bishop with special faculties appointed to assist the diocesan bishop; he possesses the right of succession (c 403 §3). **Metropolitan bishop**: a diocesan bishop who also presides over an ecclesiastical PROVINCE (c 435). See **Archbishop**. **Suffragan bishop**: a bishop of a suffragan diocese (i.e. a diocese that is not an ARCHDIOCESE) who is under the authority of the metropolitan bishop (c 436). See **Cleric**; **Consecration**; **Episcopate**; **Faculty**.

C of E. **Diocesan bishop**: the chief pastor in the diocese. He is to uphold and teach sound doctrine and to banish erroneous beliefs. He is also to be an example of 'righteous and godly living' (canon C18(1)). His episcopal rights and duties include celebrating ORDINATION and CONFIRMATION, institution to vacant PARISHES, granting LICENCES for ecclesiastical offices and holding VISITATIONS (canon C18(4)). It is the Crown who appoints him upon the advice of the prime minister. He is formally elected by the DEAN and CHAPTER of the CATHEDRAL, and his election has then to be confirmed by the ARCHBISHOP or his VICAR general (ABA s. 3). **Suffragan bishop**: a bishop nominated by the diocesan bishop to assist him in the diocese, and appointed by the Crown (SBA s. 1; canon C20(1)). In practice, a suffragan is sometimes styled 'assistant bishop' (so also are bishops resident in the diocese who may assist the diocesan). **Area bishop**: a diocesan or a suffragan bishop who is given episcopal oversight of an area within a diocese (DM s. 11). **'Flying' bishop**: a bishop who is a suffragan PROVINCIAL EPISCOPAL VISITOR within the Province of Canterbury or York and also a suffragan bishop in his archbishop's own diocese (EMAS s. 5). He provides 'alternative episcopal oversight' for parishes opposed to the ministry of women priests.

AC. Some Churches of the ANGLICAN COMMUNION have '**auxiliary bishops**' – for example, in the Indian Ocean where the office of auxiliary is equivalent to that of assistant (Indian Ocean Const., art. 14). A few Churches of the Anglican Communion have '**coadjutor bishops**'. A coadjutor is elected for a diocese when the diocesan bishop is unable to discharge the duties of office by reason of ill health, or the extent of diocesan work, or is unable to manage an orderly changeover of office. A coadjutor, unlike an auxiliary, has the right of succession. Churches which have coadjutor bishops include ECUSA, Philippines, West Indies, and Canada. See **Archbishop**; **Cleric**; **Consecration**; **Episcopate**.

BLACK-LETTER DAYS

C of E. Lesser festivals in the Church's year which are held for the commemoration of certain SAINTS. The term is used to draw a distinction between these festivals and the greater festivals which are known as RED-LETTER DAYS. See **Feast Day**.

BLASPHEMY (L *blasphemia*, Gk βλασφημία)

RC. A person commits blasphemy when he or she 'uses a public show or speech, published writings, or other media or social communication to blaspheme, seriously damage good morals, express wrongs against religion or against the Church or stir up hatred or contempt against religion or the Church (and) is to be punished with a just penalty' (c 1369).

C of E. The COMMON LAW offence of blasphemous libel is committed when a person publishes material attacking the Christian religion, God, Christ or other sacred persons, the Bible, or the DOCTRINE of the Church of England. The publication must be such as to outrage and insult the feelings of Christians (*Bowman* v. *Secular Society Ltd* [1917] AC 406, HL). The offence is one of strict liability, and so the intention to outrage and insult is not necessary (*Whitehouse* v. *Lemon and Gay News Ltd* [1979] AC 617, HL). See **Profanation**.

BONA ECCLESIASTICA (L, church goods)

RC. Temporal goods which belong to the Church (universal or particular), to the APOSTOLIC SEE or to a JURIDICAL PERSON within the Church (whether public or private) (cc 1255, 1254–1310). The Church's right of possession of temporal goods is not subject to the control of civil power (c 1254 §1). Temporal goods are held for the ordering of divine worship, the support of clergy and other ministers, and the performance of works of the sacred apostolate and of charity (c 1254 §2). See **Alienation**; *Beneplacitum*.

BRIEF (L *breve*)

RC. A pontifical letter which is usually unofficial and private in nature.

BULL (L *bulla*, seal)

RC. An official pontifical letter which is public in nature.

BURIAL

RC. A 'pious custom' which is recommended rather than CREMATION (c 1176 §3; SCHO instr. *Piam et constantem* (1963), approved by Paul VI). The deceased's funeral normally takes place in his or her 'proper parish' (c 1177 §1). Another CHURCH may be chosen with the agreement of its pastor; if so, the pastor of the 'proper parish' should be informed (c 1177 §2). Burial in churches or in ORATORIES is prohibited except in cases of popes, CARDINALS and diocesan BISHOPS (c 1242). Coadjutor and auxiliary bishops may only be buried in this way with the specific permission of the APOSTOLIC SEE. 'Notorious apostates, heretics and schismatics', those who have chosen cremation 'for anti-Christian motives', and 'other manifest sinners' are to be denied a Church funeral 'unless they gave some signs of repentance before death' (c 1184 §1).

C of E. A person who has died in the PARISH has a COMMON LAW right to be buried in the parish CHURCHYARD or cemetery (*Re Kerr* [1894] P 284 at 293; *Winstanley* v. *Manchester Overseers* [1910] AC 7 at 15). Every minister has a duty to bury parishioners and persons whose names are on the church ELECTORAL ROLL as well as those dying in the parish (canon B38(2); C of E (MP)M 1976 s. 6(1)). Persons unbaptized or who have been excommunicated or who have committed suicide may be buried in consecrated ground. However, the choice of rite for the burial service is subject to special provisions. Burial in church is not provided for under common law or CANON LAW. A FACULTY must be obtained for such a burial (see E. L. Thomas (ed.), *Baker's Law Relating to Burials* (6th edn., London, 1901), 1–2). See **Churchyard**.

C

CALUMNY (L *calumnia*)

RC. A false accusation. The Christian faithful have a right to a good reputation which is not to be unlawfully damaged, and a right to privacy which is not to be violated (c 220). Caluminous enunciation is an offence which is punishable with a just PENALTY including a CENSURE (c 1390 §2).

CAMERLENGO (L *camerarius*)

RC. A member of the College of Cardinals and a key ADMINISTRATOR when the APOSTOLIC SEE is vacant. During a vacancy the Cardinal Camerlengo with the help of three Cardinal Assistants is responsible for the care and administration of the temporal goods and rights of the HOLY SEE. He requires the vote of the College of Cardinals once and for all as regards lighter matters, and in every single case regarding more serious matters (*UDG* ch. 3 (17)). See *Sede Vacante*.

CANON (L, catalogue of sacred writings)

RC. The law of the Church. What pertains to the law of the Church as distinct from the law of the land. *CIC* contains 1752 canons which regulate the life of the Latin Church (c 1). See **Canon Law**; **Chapter**.

C of E. A means of legislating upon matters concerning the Church, which is vested in the GENERAL SYNOD (SGM s. 1(1); sched. 2, art. 6(a)(ii)). A canon requires royal assent and licence before it can be made, executed and promulged. No canon is to be made which is contrary or repugnant to the royal prerogative or the CUSTOMS, laws or statutes of the realm (SCA ss. 1, 3; SGM s. 1(3)). Canons are binding upon the clergy; since they are not confirmed by Parliament they do not bind the LAITY. Lord Hardwicke explained in *Middleton v. Crofts* (1736): 'We are all of the opinion that the Canons of 1603, not having been confirmed by Parliament, do not *proprio vigore* bind the laity; and say *proprio vigore*, by their own force and authority'. See **Canon Law**.

CANON LAW (L *ius canonicum*)

RC. Laws of the Church both divine and ECCLESIASTICAL, UNIVERSAL and PARTICULAR: also laws created by the Church in the form of

Canons, in order to manage its own internal affairs. Canon law is a set of rules which 'govern the public order of the Roman Catholic Church', and which are made up of 'norms which describe the basic structures of the Church' and 'individual regulations which constitute Church discipline' (J. A. Coriden, *An Introduction to Canon Law* (London, 1991), 3–4). For L. Örsy canon law 'springs from the will of Christ, but its minute and detailed rules come from human agents ... that is, the pope and the bishops' ('Towards a Theological Conception of Canon Law', in J. Hite and D. J. Ward (eds.), *Readings, Cases, Materials in Canon Law: A Text for Ministerial Students* (rev. edn., Minnesota, 1990) 11). Canon law is based not only upon various canons and rules but also upon Holy Scripture and Christian tradition. It is founded upon the civil law and borrows heavily from Roman law. Since the time of Gratian (twelfth century) the canon law (*corpus iuris canonici*) and the civil law (*corpus iuris civilis*) have existed independently of each other. See **Decretist**; *Decretum*.

C of E. In the narrower sense this term has been defined as 'the domestic law of the Church – the code of faith, morals and discipline' (Bishop of Chester, Debate on the Holy Table Measure 1964, HL Debates, vol. 256 (1964), 1131). Canon law in this sense has also been understood as 'directives for the guidance of the Church in ecclesiastical matters' *HLE* para. 308). In the wider sense this term is sometimes considered judicially to be part of the law of England. Garth Moore defines the term as including 'so much of the law of England as is concerned with the regulation of the affairs of the Church of England' (*MIECL* 2). In this sense canon law is viewed as including state-made law as well as church-made law that is applicable to the Church. See **Common Law**; **Ecclesiastical Law**.

Canon Penitentiary (L *canon paenetentiarius*)

RC. A Presbyter belonging to a Cathedral or collegiate Church who is appointed as confessor with Ordinary Faculties to absolve from automatic Censures which have not been declared by administrative Decree or judicial Sentence and which are not reserved to the Apostolic See (cc 508, 968). He is known as the 'priest penitentiary' (or 'the penitentiary') in a Diocese which has no Chapter of Canons.

Canonical Form (L *forma canonica*)

RC. The requirements for a valid Marriage, namely that there is Consent by the parties, there are two witnesses and the marriage is celebrated before a Priest or Deacon who has a Faculty to assist at a marriage (c 1108). See **Extraordinary Form**; **Sacramental Form**.

CANONICAL JURISPRUDENCE (L *jurisprudentia canonica*)

RC. The interpretations and application of CANON LAW as a source of divine law and human law by courts and tribunals. The principle is applied where a UNIVERSAL or PARTICULAR LAW or a CUSTOM is lacking (c 19). See **Equity.**

CANONICAL OBEDIENCE (L *obsequium canonicum*)

RC. The Christian faithful are obliged to show Christian obedience towards their pastors (i.e. BISHOPS as well as PARISH PRIESTS) as representatives of Christ concerning what they declare as teachers and determine as rulers of the Church (c 212 §1). A CLERIC is obliged to show reverence and obedience not only to his own ORDINARY but also to the Supreme Pontiff (c 273). See *Obsequium.*

C of E. According to the ancient law and usage of the Church and realm 'inferior clergy who have received authority to minister in any diocese owe canonical obedience in all things lawful and honest to the bishop of the same' (canon C1(3)). This general duty is made specific by the requirement to swear the following OATH: 'I, *AB*, do swear by Almighty God that I will pay true and canonical obedience to the Lord Bishop of *C* and his successors in all things lawful and honest: So help me God' (canon C14(3)). This oath has to be taken by a priest or DEACON at his or her ORDINATION, by an INCUMBENT when installed to a BENEFICE and by a cleric when licensed to a lectureship, preachership or stipendiary curacy. With regard to bishops, canon C14(1) states that 'Every person whose election to any bishopric is to be confirmed, or who is to be consecrated bishop or translated to any bishopric or suffragan bishopric, shall first take the oath of due obedience to the archbishop and to the metropolitical Church of the province wherein he is to exercise the episcopal office.' See **Declaration of Assent; Oath; Profession of Faith.**

CANONIZATION (L *canonizatio*)

RC. A declaration of the sainthood of a particular member of the faithful departed who has already been beatified, e.g. St Edmund Campion, St Thomas More. The process of canonization is regulated by the apostolic constitution *Divinus Perfectionis Magister* (John Paul II, 1983), which was published after *CIC* (see c 1403). A public cult is prescribed for the newly declared SAINT throughout the whole Church. See **Beatification; Promoter of the Faith; Venerable; Appendix I.**

CARDINAL (L *cardinalis*, chief)

RC. A BISHOP who is a member of the College of Cardinals which meets in CONCLAVE to elect the pope and which advises him on important matters through its CONSISTORIES. The College of Cardinals is divided into three ranks of cardinals – cardinal DEACONS, cardinal PRESBYTERS and cardinal bishops. It is presided over by a cardinal DEAN. Individually, cardinals assist the pope through the office of the Roman CURIA. A cardinal is freely selected by the pope; and a man promoted to the College of Cardinals must be at least in the order of the PRESBYTERATE (if a PRESBYTER, he must afterwards receive episcopal CONSECRATION: cc 349–59). See *Curia*.

CATECHESIS (L, Gk κατήχησις)

RC. Instruction in the Church's catechism. Pastors of souls have a duty to provide for the catechesis of Christian people in order that their faith can become 'living, explicit and productive' (c 773). The diocesan BISHOP has a responsibility to issue NORMS for catechists and to provide them with suitable instruction (c 775 §1). Members of the Conference of Bishops have competence with the approval of the APOSTOLIC SEE to ensure that catechisms are issued for their territories (c 775 §2). See **Catechist**; **Catechumen**.

C of E. The minister is to take care that children and young people of the PARISH are instructed in 'the doctrine, sacraments and discipline of Christ' as set out in the Church catechism. He or she is to give instruction or is to appoint 'godly and competent persons' to do so (canon B26). It is one of the functions of a DEACON to instruct the youth in the catechism (BCP).

CATECHIST (L *catechista*, Gk κατηχιστής)

RC. A lay person of exemplary Christian life who has undergone special training. His or her function is to present Gospel teaching and 'to engage in liturgical worship and in works of charity' (c 785 §1). See **Catechesis**.

CATECHUMEN (L *catechumenus*, Gk κατηχούμενος)

RC. An unbaptized person who seeks admission to the Church through BAPTISM. The Church has a special care for catechumens (cc 206, 788). An adult who intends to be baptized is to be admitted to the catechumenate and led stage by stage towards sacramental initiation in accordance with the instructions laid down by the Conference of BISHOPS (c 851 §1). Catechumens are also to be granted ecclesiastical funeral rites by the Church (c 1183 §1). See **Baptism**; **Catechesis**; **Catechist**.

CATHEDRAL (L *cathedra*, Gk καθέδρα)

RC and C of E. The mother CHURCH of a DIOCESE where the *cathedra* or throne of the diocesan BISHOP is found. See **Chapter**; **Dean**; **Provost**.

CAUSA MAJOR (L, important case)

RC. A matter reserved to the Supreme Pontiff, such as a cause of the CANONIZATION of a servant of God (c 1403) or the defining of dogma (c 749 §1). See **Appendix I.**

CELEBRET (L, let him celebrate)

RC. A letter of recommendation from the ORDINARY or the superior of a PRIEST which attests to the priest's ORDINATION and good standing and, therefore, his right to celebrate Mass (c 903). This letter remains valid for up to one year.

CELIBACY (L *caelibatus, coelibatus*)

RC. 'A special gift of God by which sacred ministers can adhere more easily to Christ with an undivided heart' (c 277 §1: see also *Presbyterorum Ordinis* (1965), 16). PRIESTS have an obligation to observe celibacy. Celibacy is considered appropriate for the PRIESTHOOD and has been obligatory in the Latin Church for a thousand years. The EASTERN CATHOLIC CHURCH permits the practice of married clergy; it also believes that clerical celibacy is to be greatly esteemed (*CCEO* c 373).

CENSORSHIP OF BOOKS (L *censura librorum*)

RC. A control exercised by the APOSTOLIC SEE, individual BISHOPS or the Conference of Bishops over religious writings about sacred scripture, the LITURGY, the catechism, prayer, theology, CANON LAW and other such material concerning faith or morals (cc 823–32). *Imprimatur*: the official permission of the competent ecclesiastical authority required before such books or pamphlets can be displayed, offered for sale or given away in CHURCHES (cc 824, 827). *Nihil obstat*: the judgement of the official censor that a publication contains nothing harmful to the faith and morals of the Church – only afterwards can the publication receive the *imprimatur*. *Imprimi potest*: the permission of a major superior of a religious institute also required before its members can publish writings to do with faith and morals (c 832).

CENSURE (L *censura*, judgement)

RC. A PENALTY imposed by the Church against an offending member (c 1311). A censure, or medicinal (i.e. corrective with the aim of restoring) penalty, is an EXCOMMUNICATION, INTERDICT or SUSPENSION (cc 1331–5). A censure can only be inflicted until the offender has a change of heart and is able to receive ABSOLUTION. The Church can impose various expiatory penalties which aim to remedy the social effects of an offence as well as to deter others from behaving in a similar fashion (cc 1336–8).

C of E. The result of an ecclesiastical offence committed by a Cleric. Ecclesiastical censures include deprivation, inhibition, suspension, monition and rebuke (EJM s. 49). The censure of deprivation of a Bishop or Archbishop has to be confirmed by the Sovereign (EJM s. 49(4)).

Chancel (L *cancellus*)

C of E. A part of a Church between the nave and the sanctuary where the organ, choir stalls and the Incumbent's stall or desk are usually situated. It is sometimes separated from the nave by a screen called the rood screen. The repair of the chancel is no longer the personal liability of the incumbent (EDM s. 52 (1)). An Archdeacon is required to survey all the churches, chancels and Churchyards within his or her archdeaconry (canon C22(5)).

Chancellor (L *cancellarius*, door-keeper)

RC. Usually a Priest appointed by the Bishop to be a keeper of the diocesan archives. His functions include membership of the diocesan *Curia* and being a signatory to the specified transactions (cc 482–91).

C of E. **Cathedral chancellor**: a keeper of Cathedral archives, especially cathedral statutes. **Diocesan chancellor**: a judge appointed by the diocesan bishop who presides over the Consistory Court.

Chaplain (L *capellanus*)

RC. A Presbyter who is entrusted with the pastoral care, in part at least, of a particular group or community of the Christian faithful. He is required to exercise his ministry in accordance with Universal and Particular Law (c 564). He is usually appointed by the Ordinary and is given all the Faculties his office requires (cc 565, 566: for chaplains of lay religious, chaplains to migrants, military chaplains and chaplains of non-parochial Churches see cc 567–70).

C of E. A Priest who falls within the category of unbeneficed clergy, i.e. not having a Freehold office. A chaplain who serves at a private chapel requires the Bishop's Licence or written permission to officiate (canon C8(2)): the consent of the Incumbent in whose Parish the chapel is situated is also required (canon C8(4)). A school, hospital or college chaplain also requires the bishop's licence before he or she can officiate (canons C8, C12; Extra-Parochial Ministry Measure, 1967, s. 2), but is not dependent upon the consent of the local incumbent for the exercise of his or her ministry. Provisions applying to chapels of the armed forces derive from the royal prerogative. Chaplains to the Forces are licensed by and are under the JURISDICTION of the Archbishop of Canterbury. See **Appendix II**.

CHAPTER (L *capitulum*)

RC. A college of PRIESTS who are called CANONS and are attached to a CATHEDRAL or a collegiate CHURCH in order to perform liturgical functions and duties as required by CANON LAW or by the diocesan BISHOP (cc 503–10). A **general chapter** of a religious institution represents the entire institution (c 631 §1). PROVINCES, local communities and individual members may inform the general chapter of their wishes and suggestions (c 631 §3).

C of E. The capitular body of a cathedral, with a common seal which is retained in the custody of an administrative body (CM s. 10). A chapter comprises the DEAN (or PROVOST) and the residentiary and honorary canons (CM s. 7 (a)). Its functions include the administration of the cathedral and the 'election' of a diocesan bishop by licence of the Crown under the Great Seal. A chapter cannot act without the dean unless its cathedral statutes state otherwise (CM s. 11(2)(b), (c), (d)). See *Congé d'elire*.

CHARACTER (L)

RC. *CIC* speaks about the 'character' of certain SACRAMENTS – the sacraments of BAPTISM, CONFIRMATION and ORDERS cannot be repeated because they imprint a 'character' (c 845 §1). The 'character' of these sacraments explains their effect: membership of the Church is the effect of baptism and confirmation, and the pastoral office is bestowed through the sacrament of orders.

CHARISM (L *charisma*, Gk χάρισμα, gift)

RC. God-given gifts or graces which give rise to obligations and rights. Such gifts are given primarily for the benefit of the Church and the world rather than of the individual who is bestowed with them.

CHIROGRAPHUM (L, Gk χειρόγραφον, manuscript)

RC. An APOSTOLIC LETTER entirely written by the hand of the pope.

CHRISM (L *chrisma*, Gk χρῖσμα)

RC and EC. The OIL of olives or other plants which is blessed by the BISHOP on Maundy Thursday for the administration of the SACRAMENTS of BAPTISM, CONFIRMATION, holy ORDERS and the ANOINTING OF THE SICK.

In the EASTERN CATHOLIC CHURCH the oil of chrism is to be blessed by the patriarch (*CCEO* c 693). See **Chrismation**.

C of E. Chrism is also used.

CHRISMATION (L *chrisma*, Gk χρῖσμα)

RC. Anointing with holy OIL. Chrismation with holy myron according to the tradition of the Eastern Churches is administered by a PRESBYTER either in conjunction with BAPTISM or separately (*CCEO* c 694). Candidates for sacred ORDINATION are also chrismated with holy MYRON (*CCEO* c 758 §1). See **Anointing of the Sick**; **Chrism**.

C of E. Chrismation is also performed.

CHURCH (L *ecclesia*, Gk ἐκκλησία)

RC. A 'sacred building intended for divine worship, to which the faithful have right of access for the exercise, especially the public exercise, of divine worship' (c 1214). Also, an assembly of the Christian faithful gathered for divine worship who constitute the people of God (c 204 §1). **The Catholic Church**: a community of Christians from Churches governed by the successor of Peter and the BISHOPS in communion with him (c 204 §2). **The particular Church**: the DIOCESE, 'principally': also a church which together with others makes up the universal Church (c 368). See **Particular Church**.

C of E. 'Church' means 'any church or chapel which has been consecrated for the purpose of public worship according to the rites and ceremonies of the Church of England' and includes 'a building used or intended to be used partly for the purpose of such public worship and partly for the purpose of a church hall, whether the whole building is consecrated or only such part thereof as is used or intended to be used for the purpose of such public worship' (PM s. 87(1)). Also, '"church" includes any building which is licensed for public worship according to the rites and ceremonies of the Church of England and is subject to the faculty jurisdiction' (CCEJM s. 19). **The Church of England**: a Church 'established according to the laws of this realm under the [Sovereign's] Majesty' which 'belongs to the true and apostolic Church of Christ' (canon A1). It is governed 'under the [Sovereign's] Majesty, by archbishops, bishops, deans, provosts, archdeacons, and the rest of the clergy and of the laity that bear office in the same' (canon A6). It is the established Church of the land, which is governed by the Crown in Parliament; it acknowledges the royal supremacy: the Sovereign, 'acting according to the laws of the realm, is the highest power under God in this Kingdom, and has supreme authority over all persons in all causes, as well ecclesiastical as civil' (canon A7). The internal governance of the Church is carried out through a hierarchical structure of synodical government with the GENERAL SYNOD at its head. See **Diocese**; **Synod**.

CHURCH RATE

C of E. A voluntary rate which the PAROCHIAL CHURCH COUNCIL is empowered to raise for any purpose connected with church affairs (including its own administrative expenses and any legal costs it incurs) (see PCC(P)M s. 7(ii)). Compulsory church rates were abolished (save in exceptional cases) by the Compulsory Church Rate Abolition Act, 1868.

CHURCHING OF WOMEN

RC. This service has been replaced by the blessing of the parents and their child in the sanctuary at the end of the baptismal celebration. When BAPTISM is postponed until the parents are able to make the baptismal promises a simple blessing may be given. If the mother cannot attend the baptism a separate form of blessing is provided (*Rituale Romanum: De Benedictionibus* (1984), pt. 1, nos. 236–57).

C of E. A service which is intended to be the first public service to be attended by a woman after childbirth, at which she makes an act of thanksgiving for her safe delivery. The full title of the service according to BCP is 'The Thanksgiving of Women after Childbirth, commonly called The Churching of Women'. According to the RUBRICS she is to come to the PARISH CHURCH decently apparelled and is to kneel down at a place accustomed or prescribed by the ORDINARY. If the service includes Holy Communion she is to partake. The service is to be performed by a PRIEST to whom the woman is to offer the accustomed offering (BCP, rubrics before the Churching of Women). The ASB includes a form of service of 'Thanksgiving for the Birth of a Child' and also of 'Thanksgiving after Adoption'. All three services are to be performed by the minister.

CHURCHWARDEN

C of E. An officer of the BISHOP and custodian of CHURCH property in the PARISH; they are usually two in number (C(A and R)M s. 1(1)). To qualify for appointment they must either reside in the parish or have their names on the parish ELECTORAL ROLL (ibid. s. 1(2)). They must also be communicant members of the church and over twenty-one years of age (ibid. s. 1(3)). Their responsibilities include actively participating in the Church's mission in the parish, maintaining order and decency in the church and CHURCHYARD, and keeping and revising an inventory of church plate, ornaments and other movable goods (canon E1). They are also to provide enough bread and wine for Holy Communion (canon B17(1)) and are responsible for completing the ARCHDEACON's Articles of Enquiry in readiness for his VISITATION (canon G6). See **Rural Dean**.

CHURCHYARD

RC. The Church has its own cemeteries, or at least spaces 'duly blessed and reserved for the deceased faithful' in civil cemeteries. If neither is available, individual graves are to be blessed (c 1240 §§1, 2). The Church recommends BURIAL, although CREMATION is not forbidden unless it is chosen for a reason which is unchristian (c 1176 §3). A non-Catholic may be given an ecclesiastical funeral provided that the local ORDINARY considers such action to be prudent, such action is not contrary to the will of the deceased, and the deceased's own minister is unavailable (c 1183 §3). ROMAN PONTIFFS, CARDINALS and diocesan BISHOPS may be buried in their 'proper' church (c 1242). See **Burial**.

C of E. The FREEHOLD of the churchyard, as curtailed by the FACULTY JURISDICTION, vests in the INCUMBENT. Its maintenance is the responsibility of the PCC. CHURCHWARDENS have a duty to maintain order and decency in the churchyard, especially during divine services (canon E1(4)). Parishioners and persons whose names are on the ELECTORAL ROLL, as well as those dying in the PARISH, have a right to be buried or to have their ashes interred in the parish churchyard (C of E (MP)M 1976 s. 6(1); canon B 38(2)). See **Curtilage**; **Electoral Roll**.

CIRCUMSTANCE (L *circumstantia*)

RC. A factor which affects IMPUTABILITY in the commission of an ecclesiastical offence. Imputability is removed when the person involved is under sixteen years of age or when the person was ignorant of violating a law or PRECEPT, or when he or she acted out of grave fear, or in legitimate self-defence, or lacked the use of reason, etc. (c 1323). Factors which diminish imputability include imperfect use of reason, drunkenness, passion, provocation and ignorance (c 1324). Imputability is heightened by such factors as the repetition of an offence after the declaration of a PENALTY, and the abuse of authority (c 1326). See **Delict**.

CITATION (L *citatio*)

RC. A judicial summons served upon the RESPONDENT or the respondents of a petition. The DECREE of citation must either call into court or cite the other parties of the joinder of issues. The judge is to require the parties to respond in writing or to present themselves personally in court (cc 1507–12). A citation, in a broader sense, also refers to the notification of the DEFENDER OF THE BOND and the PROMOTER OF JUSTICE in cases where their presence is required. See *Litis Contestatio*.

C of E. A notice issued by the diocesan CHANCELLOR which states that an application has been made for a FACULTY, and which makes parishioners and others aware of their right to object (FJR r. 15(1)). It must be displayed both inside and outside the CHURCH for a continuous period of not less than fourteen days (including at least one Sunday when worship is held in the church) (FJR r. 5(4)). The diocesan chancellor may, in addition, require a citation to be served on particular persons, bodies and societies, or for a notice of citation to be published in local newspapers (FJR rr. 12(1), (2), (3)). See **Consistory Court**.

CLEMENTINES (L *constitutiones Clementinae*, constitutions of Clement)

RC. A collection of DECRETALS divided into five books and containing the Constitutions of Pope Clement V (1305–14). They were published by his successor Pope John XXII in 1317. The Clementines formed part of the *Corpus Iuris Canonici* (1500) put together by the canonist John Chapuis. See *Corpus*; **Decretalist**.

CLERIC (L *clericus*, Gk κληρικός)

RC. A person within the three grades of the SACRAMENT of ORDERS; one who is a DEACON, PRESBYTER or BISHOP (c 1009 §1). See **Diaconate; Episcopate; Presbyterate**.

C of E. A person in holy orders; one who has been ordained bishop, PRIEST or deacon (canon C1). See **Diaconate; Episcopate; Priesthood**.

CLOISTER (L *claustrum*)

RC. The enclosure of a religious house, governed by appropriate law. **Common cloister**: parts of a religious house which are reserved for its religious members only. Outsiders may not enter these parts save in exceptional circumstances (c 667 §1). **Stricter cloister**: the regimen observed in monasteries which are contemplative in nature (c 667 §2). **Papal cloister**: the regimen observed by monasteries of nuns which are completely ordered to the contemplative life. NORMS for papal cloisters are enacted by the APOSTOLIC SEE (c 667 §3). **Constitutional cloister**: the regimen observed by monasteries of nuns who perform apostolic work. It is defined in the monasteries' CONSTITUTIONS and is adapted to their character (c 667 §3). The diocesan BISHOP has the FACULTY of entering, for a just reason, the enclosure of nuns whose monasteries are situated in his DIOCESE; he can, for a grave reason,

and with the consent of the abbess, permit others to be admitted to the
enclosure; furthermore, he can permit the nuns to leave the enclosure
for whatever time is necessary (c 677 §4); see J. E. Gallen, *Canon
Law for Religious* (New York, 1983). For norms governing the entering
and leaving of a cloister, see SCRIS: *Venite Seorsum* (1969); see also
Paul VI: *Ecclesiae Sanctae* (1966); Vatican II: *Perfectae Caritatis*
(1965).

C of E. 'Enclosed' communities, like other religious communities,
follow their own rules as set out in their constitutions. An Advisory
Council on the Relations of Bishops and Religious Communities serves
the PROVINCES of Canterbury and York. This council is responsible to
the two ARCHBISHOPS, and to the House of Bishops of the GENERAL
SYNOD. Its functions include advising the bishops upon matters
which arise concerning the constitutions and rule of communities, and
giving advice to communities on matters referred to it by them. See
A Directory of the Religious Life (4th edn., London, 1990).

COADJUTOR (L *Coadjutor episcopus*, an assistant bishop)

RC. A BISHOP with special FACULTIES appointed to assist the diocesan
bishop and possessing the right of succession (cc 403–11).

AC. A few Churches of the ANGLICAN COMMUNION have coadjutor
bishops. See **Bishop**.

CODEX (L *caudex*, a writing, code of laws)

RC. A book containing an official collection of laws divided into groups
of CANONS. The Codex of Justinian replaced the earliest codes – those
of Gregory (291), Hermogenianus (295) and Theodosianus (435). It
was part of the *Corpus Iuris Civilis*. The present *Codex Iuris Canonici*
(1983) containing 1,752 canons replaces the 1917 Codex. See *Corpus*.

C of E. The codification of the present Canons Ecclesiastical (5th edn.
1993) by the CONVOCATIONS OF CANTERBURY AND YORK in 1964 and
1969 replaced nearly the whole of the code of 1603 with the exception
of canon 113 on CONFESSION. Since 1970 the GENERAL SYNOD has made
further amendments and revocations. The term 'code' is used by some
Churches of the ANGLICAN COMMUNION to denote a collection of canons.
Scotland has a code of canons; New Zealand has a CONSTITUTION and
a code of canons. **Code of Practice**: informal administrative rules
which serve as directions or guidelines and which are designed to
supplement the formal law. In the Church of England these rules
supplement synodical MEASURES, e.g. Pastoral Measure, 1983; Code
of Recommended Practice, 1983. Codes of practice are usually
recommendatory rather than binding; however, according to Papua

New Guinea, Diocese of Port Moresby, canon 10(3): 'All clergy . . .
are subject to lawful obedience to the . . . Bishop's Guidelines.'

COGNATION (L *cognatio*)

RC. Blood relationship through the female line, as opposed to AGNATION
which is through the male line. There is no distinction in CANON LAW
between the two expressions of CONSANGUINITY: those who are related
in the direct line cannot validly contract MARRIAGE between themselves
(c 1094). The term is also used to refer to blood relationship in general.
See **Agnation**; **Impediment**.

COLLATION

C of E. The INSTITUTION of a PRIEST as the INCUMBENT of a PARISH where
PATRONAGE vests in the BISHOP (canon C9).

COLLEGE OF BISHOPS (L *episcopale collegium*)

RC. This college, with the pope as its head, exercises full and supreme
power over the universal Church. Members of the college are in
hierarchical communion with the pope as well as with each other; the
college, therefore, cannot act without the pope (c 336). In matters of
faith and morals the college, gathered together in an ECUMENICAL
COUNCIL, possesses infallible teaching authority. When dispersed,
individual BISHOPS also possess the same authority when they act in
communion with each other as a college and with the pope as its head,
provided they are in unanimous agreement (c 749 §2; c 337). See
Magisterium.

COMMISSARY

C of E. A person appointed by the BISHOP to act for him. Such a person
is commissioned by the bishop to do certain work in a particular area
for a specified time. A commissary may be appointed by the bishop to
institute a CLERIC (see canon C17(3)). On such occasions the commissary is given all the powers the bishop might have used had he
been present. For Commissary Court and commissary in general, see
Consistory Court; for Archbishop of Canterbury's Commissary, see
Court of Faculties.

COMMON LAW (L *ius commune*)

RC. Law and CUSTOM which is common to the universal Church.

C of E. The unwritten customary law of the land which applies to either
general or ECCLESIASTICAL LAW. As Lord Blackburn explained,
'ecclesiastical law is not a foreign law. It is part of the general law of

England – of the common law – in that wider sense' (*Mackonochie* v. *Lord Penzance* (1881) 6 AppCas 424 at 446). See **Canon Law**.

COMMUNICATIO IN SACRIS (L)

RC. A sharing in sacred things. A participation in sacred rites with other Christians, especially a sharing in the reception of the SACRAMENTS by Catholics from non-Catholic ministers, and non-Catholics from Catholic ministers (cc 844, 1356; *CCEO* cc 908, 1440). See **Ecumenism**; **Eucharist**; **Intercommunion**.

COMMUNICATIONES (L, information)

RC. The official journal of the Pontifical Commission for the Revision of the Code of Canon Law (1969–83). The commission later became known as the Pontifical Commission for the Authentic Interpretation of the Code. It is known today as the *Pontificum Consilium de Legum Textibus Interpretandis* (see *PB*). See **Appendix III**.

COMPETENCE (L *competentia*, official qualification, competence)

RC. The right of a tribunal to judge a case. The competent FORUM, territorially, is (i) the tribunal of the RESPONDENT's place of DOMICILE or quasi-domicile (c 1407 §3); (ii) the tribunal of the place where a contract was made or where a litigated thing is located, whenever an action is directed against the thing or whenever it is a question of damages (cc 1410, 1411); (iii) in penal cases, the tribunal of the place where the offence occurred (c 1412). The tribunals of the APOSTOLIC SEE have universal territorial competence. Certain tribunals have the right to judge in certain cases, e.g. in contentious cases BISHOPS are judged by the Roman ROTA; CARDINALS and LEGATES of the Apostolic See are judged by the ROMAN PONTIFF; and the Roman Pontiff is judged by no one (cc 1404; 1405 §§1, 3).

COMPROMISE (L *compromissum*)

RC. (1) An agreement by parties to settle a dispute or to refer the matter to ARBITRATION, in order to avoid judicial contention (cc 1713–16). See **Arbitration**; *Transactio*. (2) A mode of effecting an ELECTION. A person or persons may be commissioned by electors or an electoral college to elect, by FACULTY, in their name (cc 174, 175).

CONCLAVE (L, room)

RC. A formal gathering of the College of Cardinals for the specific purpose of electing a pope. CARDINALS must be under eighty years of age to participate in the ELECTION. The procedure for election is set out in the apostolic constitution *Universi Dominici Gregis* (John Paul II, 1996). See **Consistory.**

CONCORDAT (L, he agrees)

RC. An agreement made between the APOSTOLIC SEE and a sovereign state, controlling matters of common interest. It sets out Church–state conventions such as the organization of DIOCESES in legal form. Such an agreement is subject to the NORMS of international law and is outside the scope of *CIC*. The first important concordat was the **Concordat of Worms** (1122) made between Pope Callixtus II and the emperor Henry V, which settled the Investiture Contest – BISHOPS were to be elected by the clergy and people rather than by the pope and emperor. Other famous concordats include that of 1801 with Napoleon Bonaparte of France, and that of 1929 with Italy. Concordats are usually signed by the pope himself rather than by a general council of the Church.

C of E. **Ecumenical concordat**: a means of determining relations between Churches of the ANGLICAN COMMUNION and other Churches. Examples are: (i) The Concordat of Full Communion (1961) between the Mar Thoma Church and (the former) Anglican Church of India, Pakistan, Burma and Ceylon; the Mar Thoma Syrian Church of Malabar is now in full communion with the united Churches in India and Pakistan; (ii) The Concordat of Full Communion (1961) between ECUSA and the Lusitanian Church, which was integrated as a full member of the Anglican Communion in 1980. See **Ecumenism.**

CONDITION (L *condicio*, particular situation)

RC. **Conditional marriage**: a MARRIAGE based upon a past condition (e.g. that a spouse has not been previously married) or a present condition (e.g. that a spouse is not immoral) is valid provided that the condition still exists (c 1102 §2). Such conditions in a legal agreement between the parties require the written permission of the local ORDINARY (c 1102 §3). A marriage based upon a future condition (e.g. subsequently having children) is invalid (c 1102 §1). **Conditional conferral of sacraments**: the SACRAMENTS of BAPTISM, CONFIRMATION or ORDER may be conferred conditionally if there is doubt whether they have been truly or validly conferred (c 845 §2). These sacraments cannot be repeated (c 845 §1).

C of E. If there is doubt about the baptism of a candidate for confirmation the CLERIC has to administer conditional baptism (canon B27(5)).

CONFESSION (L *confessio*)

RC. **General confession**: a corporate act during the Mass. **Private confession:** a PRESBYTER is obliged to hear confessions in cases of 'urgent necessity' and 'in danger of death' (c 986 §2). Confession of serious sin is obligatory (c 989). The 'seal of the confessional' is 'inviolable' (cc 983, 959–89).

C of E. **General confession**: a corporate act during divine service. **Private confession**: an individual act of the penitent, in the presence of a PRIEST, which is not obligatory. The 'seal' of the confessional must not be broken by the priest (canon B29; see the *proviso* to canon 113 of the Canons Ecclesiastical of 1603).

CONFIRMATION (L *confirmatio,* a confirming, fortifying)

RC. A SACRAMENT of the Church. 'By it the baptised continue their path of Christian initiation. They are enriched with the gift of the Holy Spirit, and are more closely linked to the Church. They are made strong and more firmly obliged by word and deed to witness to Christ and to spread and defend the faith' (c 879). The diocesan BISHOP has a responsibility to ensure that 'confirmation is conferred upon his subjects who duly and reasonably request it' (c 885 §1). The diocesan bishop administers confirmation (or another bishop if he cannot fulfil his obligation); in cases of NECESSITY he may grant to one or more PRIESTS a FACULTY to administer confirmation (c 884 §1). The faithful are usually to be confirmed 'at about the age of discretion' (c 891) provided that they have been 'suitably instructed' and are 'properly disposed and able to renew the baptismal promises' (c 889 §2). Each candidate is required to have a SPONSOR whose function is to ensure that the candidate 'behaves as a true witness of Christ and faithfully fulfils the duties inherent in this sacrament' (c 892). The godparent at BAPTISM is expected to act as sponsor at confirmation (c 893 §2). See **Character**.

C of E. A rite which is an integral part of the process of initiation. The promises made at baptism are confirmed by the candidate. The gifts of the Holy Spirit which he or she receives during the service enable the candidate to live the Christian life to the full. According to the rite the bishop is to confirm by laying hands upon 'children and other persons who have been baptised and instructed in the Christian faith' (canon B27(1)). A minister having the cure of souls is obliged to 'seek out' candidates for confirmation and to use his best endeavours to instruct them in the Christian faith and life (canon B27(2)). Candidates must have 'come to years of discretion' and be able to say the Creed, the Lord's Prayer and the Ten Commandments, and be able to 'render an account of their faith according to the Catechism' (canon B27(3)). See **Baptism**.

CONGÉ D'ÉLIRE (F, permission to elect)

C of E. The licence under the Great Seal which the Crown grants the DEAN and CHAPTER or a CATHEDRAL chapter in order to proceed to the ELECTION of a BISHOP. A letter missive given under the signet is sent with the name of the person to be elected (ABA s. 3).

CONSANGUINITY (L *consanguinitas*)

RC. The blood relationship which exists between persons who are descended one from another. **Direct line of consanguinity**: the line between ancestors and descendants (e.g. parents, children, grandchildren) wherein consanguinity is determined by degree (e.g. father and son are related in the first degree: c 108). The IMPEDIMENT of consanguinity prohibits MARRIAGE between all ancestors and descendants, whether related legitimately or naturally (c 1091 §1). **Collateral or parallel line of consanguinity**: the line between persons of common stock (e.g. brothers and sisters) wherein marriage is invalid up to and including the fourth degree (i.e. between first cousins; see c 1091 §2). See **Affinity**.

C of E. No person is allowed to marry within the prohibited degrees: 'all marriages purported to be made within the said degrees are void' (canon B31). See **Impediment**.

CONSECRATION (L *consecratio*)

RC. A divine act whereby a PRESBYTER is ordained to the EPISCOPATE. At his CONSECRATION (or episcopal ORDINATION) a PRIEST receives the divine gifts of teaching, governing and sanctifying which enable him to function as a BISHOP in his DIOCESE (c 375). During the service the elected bishop makes a PROFESSION OF FAITH and swears an OATH of loyalty to the APOSTOLIC SEE (c 380). See **Dedication**.

C of E. The elected bishop at his consecration makes a declaration of faith and swears an oath of due obedience to his ARCHBISHOP. He also promises to live a sober, righteous and godly life. As a shepherd to his people, he is to watch over them and feed them. He is to minister discipline tempered with mercy (BCP). **Consecration of Church property**: the setting aside of a building or CHURCHYARD through a religious ceremony performed by the bishop and, in law, by his signing the SENTENCE of consecration. Consecrated land is to be used for sacred purposes in perpetuity. The diocesan bishop has the power to remove the legal effects of consecration in circumstances where '(*a*) the building or land is not held or controlled by any ecclesiastical corporation . . . or by any Diocesan Board of Finance; and (*b*) no purpose will be served by its remaining subject to the legal effects of consecration' (CCEJM s. 22 (1)). Consecrated land may also be freed for secular purposes by Act of Parliament or MEASURE (*Re St Mary the Virgin, Woodkirk* [1969] 1 WLR 1867; *Re St John's, Chelsea* [1962] 1 WLR 706 at 714).

CONSENT (MARITAL) (L *consensus matrimonialis*)

RC. Under matrimonial law consent is essential, and the parties must be free to marry each other (c 1057). **Conditional consent**: a ground for NULLITY of MARRIAGE. A marriage entered into subject to a CONDITION concerning the future is invalid; if the condition concerns the past or the present the marriage is invalid if the condition is not in writing or is not fulfilled (c 1102).

CONSISTORY (L *consistorium*, place of assembly)

RC. A formal gathering of the College of Cardinals convoked by the pope (c 353). There are three kinds of consistories: public, semi-public and private. Both **public** and **semi-public consistories** are involved with different stages in the process of CANONIZATION. It is at the public consistory that the pope receives foreign sovereigns, heads of state, ambassadors, etc. and where he confers the 'red hat' upon new CARDINALS. **Private consistories** deal with the most important matters affecting the papacy. See **Conclave**.

CONSISTORY COURT (L *consistorium*, place of assembly)

C of E. The BISHOP's court in the DIOCESE (EJM s. 1). The diocesan CHANCELLOR presides over it. The chancellor is appointed by the bishop after consultation with the Lord Chancellor and the DEAN OF THE ARCHES (EJM s. 2(1A): in the diocese of Canterbury the court is known as the Commissary Court and the chancellor as the Commissary-General). The court has JURISDICTION over all PARISH CHURCHES in the diocese (CCEJM s. 11(1)). Proceedings against clergy over ecclesiastical offences are dealt with in the Consistory Court. The court's main function is to exercise the FACULTY jurisdiction (EJM ss. 6, 7; FJR rr. 9, 11, 12).

CONSTITUTION (L *constitutio*, regulation)

RC. A solemn legislative text issued by the pope (an 'Apostolic Constitution') or by a Council (a 'Conciliar Constitution'). See *Motu Proprio*. *The Apostolic Constitutions*: a fourth-century manual of Church order compiled in the neighbourhood of Antioch. Early canonical decisions can also be found in documents such as the *Didache*, the *Didascalia* and the *Traditio Apostolica*, as well as in the decisions of regional councils such as the Council of Elvira (AD 300).

Religious constitutions: the internal legislative texts of religious institutes. The Constitutions of such institutes must contain fundamental Norms about their governance and the discipline of their members, etc. (c 587).

C of E. A body of legal rules and regulations pertaining to the Church and embodied in a written document. The rules and regulations of the Church are to be found in its Canons and Measures which have been passed by the General Synod and which have been promulgated by Parliament. Whilst the Church of England has no formal written constitution, most Churches of the Anglican Communion do. See **Canon; Canon Law; General Synod; Measure; Promulgation**.

Contemplative Life: see **Cloister.**

Contraception

RC. An artificial means of birth control. The Church draws a distinction between contraception and natural family planning. It is regarded as an intrinsic disorder (i.e. a disorder in itself). 'Each and every marriage act' is required to be open to the transmission of life (Paul VI: Encyclical Letter *Humanae Vitae* (1968), 11). Any means of birth control which directly interrupts the generative process, once it has begun, is excluded. Only the 'rhythm method' of birth control is licit. It is immoral for a husband or wife to deprive or hinder the procreation of new life (Pius XII: Allocution to midwives (1957). Contraception leads to a falsifying of the true meaning of conjugal love (John Paul II: Apostolic exhortation *Familiaris Consortio* (1981), 32).

Contumacy (L *contumacia*)

RC. Persistent contempt of Church authority. The contempt must be clear before a Censure can be validly inflicted. Furthermore, with regard to *Ferendae Sententiae* censure the offender must have been warned at least once in advance and have been given a suitable time to repent (c 1347 §1). The offender is said to have withdrawn from contumacy upon genuine repentance and also repair of the damage or scandal caused (or an earnest promise to do so: c 1347 §2). See *Latae Sententiae*.

Convalidation (L *convalidatio matrimonii*)

RC. A legal remedy to validate a Marriage when Consent is invalid. **Simple convalidation** (cc 1156–60): a private or public renewal of consent by the spouses (or one of them) according to Canonical Form: the exchange of consent brings the marriage Covenant into existence. This procedure is applied where consent is invalid owing to the presence of an undispensed IMPEDIMENT, or defective consent or lack of canonical form. **Radical sanation** (cc 1161–5): action taken by the APOSTOLIC SEE or the local ORDINARY (or their delegates) to convalidate a marriage. This action makes the original consent valid with the result that the marriage is deemed to have existed from the beginning, and its effects are retroactive to the time of the initial consent (c 1161). A marriage which is invalid owing to a canonical impediment or a lack of canonical form can be sanated provided consent to the marriage by the spouses still exists. A marriage which is invalid owing to an impediment of natural or divine law can only be sanated when the impediment no longer exists (cc 1162–3).

CONVOCATION OF AMERICAN CHURCHES IN EUROPE

AC. A community of Episcopal Churches on the European Continent, comparable to, but smaller than, the Church of England Diocese in Europe. This community is under the JURISDICTION of the Presiding Bishop of ECUSA, who exercises this jurisdiction through a BISHOP-in-charge, comparable to a Church of England suffragan bishop. See **Parallel Episcopal Jurisdiction**.

CONVOCATIONS OF CANTERBURY AND YORK

C of E. The two ancient representative assemblies of the clergy of the PROVINCES of Canterbury and York. Both convocations sit as two Houses – Upper and Lower. The Upper House consists of the ARCH-BISHOP and the diocesan BISHOPS. The Lower House consists of DEANS of CATHEDRALS, ARCHDEACONS, PROCTORS elected by the diocesan clergy, and certain university representatives. The Lower House, at the start of each convocation, has to elect one of its members to be PROLOCUTOR. Nearly all the functions of convocation were transferred to the GENERAL SYNOD – which consists of Houses of Bishops, Clergy and LAITY – by the Synodical Government Measure, 1969. Each convocation may still meet separately to formally consider Church matters in its own province.

CORPORATION SOLE

C of E. An ecclesiastical corporation in which Church property is vested. In law such a corporation has a permanent capacity to hold property, which is unaffected by a change in the holder of a particular office. Examples of corporations sole are ARCHBISHOPS, BISHOPS, CANONS, ARCHDEACONS and INCUMBENTS. An incumbent has a FREEHOLD interest in the emoluments of a BENEFICE until his or her death, or vacation of the benefice.

CORPUS (L, a body, collection)

RC. A body of law comprising a collection of canonical NORMS as opposed to a code with a structure and list of CANONS. *Corpus Iuris Canonici*: a body of law drawn from CUSTOMS and DECREES. It comprises Gratian (1140), Gregory IX (1234), the *Liber Sextus* of Boniface VIII (1298), the *CLEMENTINES* of Clement V (1313), the *Extravagantes* of John XXII (1325) and the *Extravagantes Communes*. *Corpus Iuris Civilis*: the body of Roman secular law as set out in collective form by Justinian in the sixth century. It comprises the *Codex*, the *Digest*, the *Institutes* and *Novels*. See **Codex**.

COURT OF ECCLESIASTICAL CAUSES RESERVED

C of E. A Church court established by the EJM. It hears cases where the offences involve DOCTRINE, ritual or ceremonial. It also hears appeals from the CONSISTORY COURTS in FACULTY cases involving matters of doctrine, ritual or ceremonial. Furthermore, suits of *DUPLEX QUERELA* are heard by the court.

COURT OF FACULTIES

C of E. The court of the Archbishop of Canterbury. Historically it exercised vestiges of the legatine powers which belonged to the Archbishop at the time of the Reformation, i.e. the making of LICENCES, DISPENSATIONS and FACULTIES 'for causes not being contrary or repugnant to the Holy Scriptures and laws of God' (25 Hen. VIII c. 21). The court was very active during and after the Reformation period, as is evident from its patent rolls and faculty and ACT registers. Nowadays the court exercises JURISDICTION over the appointment and removal of ecclesiastical NOTARIES and public notaries. It also grants faculties (i.e. privileges or special dispensations), including licences to marry and LAMBETH DEGREES. This power to grant licences and dispensations is subject to confirmation by the Crown, and they have force and authority throughout England (canon C17(7)). The DEAN OF THE ARCHES is also Master of the Faculties of the Archbishop of Canterbury. The court has no judicial power. See **Commissary**.

COVENANT (L *foedus*)

RC. In Holy Scripture the pact which exists between God and His people. *CIC* describes matrimony as a covenant between two baptized persons which is ordered towards the good of the spouses and the procreation and education of children (c 1055 §1). Such a covenant has been given the dignity of a SACRAMENT by Christ (*Gaudium et Spes*, 47–52). See **Marriage**.

C of E. A form of ecumenical agreement between the Church of England and some other Church or Churches in order to seek unity. Many Churches of the ANGLICAN COMMUNION employ this form. Covenants are governed by rules about ecumenical development laid down by the LAMBETH CONFERENCE (LC 1968, res. 47). **Covenanting**: a scheme of financial giving towards the PARISH for tax-paying members. It provides the parish with the extra benefit of income tax repaid at no additional cost to the members. Systematic giving throughout the year is ensured by the covenanting of weekly collections through an envelope scheme. See **Quota**.

CREMATION (L *crematio*)

RC. Cremation is permitted so long as it is for reasons which are consistent with Christian teaching. BURIAL, however, is recommended (c 1176 (3)).

C of E. Cremation is lawful (canon B38(3)). There is the same right of burial of cremated remains as there is of a corpse in the PARISH (C of E (MP)M 1992 s. 3). A corpse and cremated remains are treated alike in the Church's CANON LAW (*Re Atkins* [1989] 1 All ER 14 at 16 per Quentin Edwards Ch).

CURATE

C of E. An unbeneficed clergyman or clergywoman appointed by the diocesan BISHOP to assist the INCUMBENT of a BENEFICE or to be responsible for a PARISH which lacks an incumbent. See **Licence**.

CURIA (L, building used for assemblies)

RC. A group of various offices and persons to assist the pope or a BISHOP in their ministry of governance. The **Roman** *Curia*: 'the complex of dicasteries and institutes which help the Roman Pontiff in the exercise of his supreme pastoral function for the good and service of the whole world and of particular churches' (*PB* art. 1; see also cc 360, 361). The *Curia* is made up of DICASTERIES and institutes divided into: the Secretariat of State, congregations, tribunals, pontifical councils, offices, other institutes of the Roman *Curia*, ADVOCATES, and institutes pertaining to the HOLY SEE (*PB*). See **Appendix III**. The **Diocesan** *Curia*: members are appointed by the diocesan bishop. The most important members are the VICAR general and the episcopal vicar (cc 469–94). See **Dicastery**.

C of E. The Church has a system of synodical government. The supreme legislative and deliberative body is the GENERAL SYNOD (SGM s. 2(1) and sched. 2 at 6). The diocesan bishop governs his DIOCESE with the aid of ARCHDEACONS and RURAL DEANS, whom he appoints, and a structure of diocesan committees. Church matters in the diocese and deaneries are implemented by the diocesan and deanery SYNODS respectively. There is also a diocesan registrar and a diocesan CHANCELLOR (see canons C22, C23). See **Synod**.

CURTILAGE

C of E. A piece of ground lying near and belonging to a property and included within the same fence or wall. For example, the curtilage of a vicarage or the curtilage of a CHURCH.

CUSTOM (L *consuetudo*, usage)

RC. Custom falls into three categories: *secundum legem* (according to the law), *praeter legem* (beyond the law) and *contra legem* (contrary to the law). For a custom to be a rule it must be approved by the legislator, it must be reasonable, it must have been observed by a community capable of receiving a law, and with the intention of introducing a law for thirty continuous years; such a custom has the force of law even if it is *praeter legem* or *contra legem* so long as the legislator gives specific approval to the custom (c 26). Existing customs are entirely suppressed if contrary to *CIC* (c 5 §1). Customs which are centenary or immemorial are valid so long as they are tolerated (c 5 §1). Existing universal or particular customs which are *praeter legem* are to be preserved or maintained (c 5 §2). Custom is seen as the best interpreter of laws (c 27). Custom *praeter legem* or *contra legem* is revoked by a contrary custom of law. A UNIVERSAL LAW does not usually revoke a particular custom (c 28).

C of E. **Pre-Reformation canon law**: a custom could be established by long and continued use: such custom had the status of law. **Post-Reformation canon law**: in order to become a part of the ECCLESIASTICAL LAW a usage of pre-Reformation canon law is required to have been recognized, continued and acted upon since the Reformation (*Bishop of Exeter* v. *Marshall* (1868) LR 3, HL 17; *Re St Mary's, Westwell* [1968] 1 WLR 513). **Custom *praeter legem***: where usage can permit something where there is no positive law to the contrary (e.g. the use of hymns in divine service, the taking of collection at Matins or Evensong). Before the Reformation between ten and twenty years was sufficient to create a rule when no other rule was in force; in modern ecclesiastical law between two hundred and three hundred years seems necessary to create a permitted usage (*Marson* v. *Unmack* [1923] P 163 at 167–8). **Custom *contra legem***:

its place in modern ecclesiastical law seems to have disappeared in the light of statute and case law (SCA ss. 1, 3; *Archbishop of Canterbury* [1902] 2 KB 503; *Kensit* v. *Dean and Chapter of St Paul's* [1905] 2 KB 249).

D

DAILY OFFICES

C of E. Morning and Evening Prayer. BISHOPS, PRIESTS and DEACONS are obliged to say Morning and Evening Prayer daily except in cases of sickness or some other urgent matter (canon C26(i)). Notice of the saying of the daily office in CHURCH is given by tolling the bell, or other appropriate means (canon B1(2): for the daily offices in CATHEDRAL churches see canon B10).

DEACON (L *diaconus*, Gk διάκονος)

RC. A CLERIC who belongs to the sacred ORDER of deacon. He is to participate in the celebration of divine worship (c 835 §3). He is to exercise the *diaconia* of LITURGY, word and charity. His duties include administering Holy Baptism, distributing Holy Communion, reading the Scriptures, presiding over worship and prayer, taking the *viaticum* to the dying (*LG* 29). The PERMANENT DIACONATE was restored at Vatican II.

C of E. His or her duties include the reading of Scripture in church, assisting the PRIEST at divine worship and visiting the sick – see ORDINAL. A deacon must make an OATH of CANONICAL OBEDIENCE to the ORDINARY and also a DECLARATION OF ASSENT (canons C14, C15). There is no provision for a permanent diaconate. See **Cleric**.

DEAN (L *decanus*)

C of E. A PRIEST who is appointed to a CATHEDRAL preferment within the meaning of PM s. 85(5). A dean has the cure of souls of the clergy who comprise the cathedral CHAPTER. The duties of a dean are set out in canon C21: to diligently observe the statutes and CUSTOMS of the cathedral, the ECCLESIASTICAL LAW of the land, and the directions of the BISHOP at his VISITATION (canon C21(2)); to reside in the cathedral, to preach God's word and to carry out such other duties as are prescribed by law and the statutes of the cathedral (canon C21 (3)); to act with reverence, care and solemnity during divine services in the cathedral to the honour and glory of God (canon C21(4)). See **Chapter**; **Provost**.

DEAN OF THE ARCHES

C of E. A judge who presides over the Court of Arches, the provincial court of appeal in the PROVINCE of Canterbury. The same judge also presides over the Chancery Court of York, the provincial court of appeal in the province of York, where he is known as the Auditor (EJM s. 3(2)(*a*)). He is appointed by the Archbishops of Canterbury and York jointly, with the approval of the Crown. If a layman, he is required to be a communicant (EJM s. 3(3)). See **Court of Faculties**.

DECLARATION OF ASSENT

C of E. A BISHOP or suffragan bishop at his CONSECRATION and a PRIEST or DEACON before his or her ORDINATION is required to make a Declaration of Assent as set out in canon C15(1):

'Preface

The Church of England is part of the One, Holy, Catholic and Apostolic Church worshipping the one true God Father, Son and Holy Spirit. It professes the faith uniquely revealed in the Holy Scriptures and set forth in the catholic creeds, which faith the Church is called upon to proclaim afresh in each generation. Led by the Holy Spirit, it has borne witness to Christian truth in its historic formularies, the thirty-nine Articles of Religion, the Book of Common Prayer and the Ordering of Bishops, Priests and Deacons. In the declaration you are about to make will you affirm your loyalty to this inheritance of faith as your inspiration and guidance under God in bringing the grace and truth of Christ to this generation and making Him known to those in your care?

Declaration of Assent

I, *AB*, do so affirm, and accordingly declare my belief in the faith which is revealed in the Holy Scriptures and set forth in the catholic creeds and to which the historic formularies of the Church of England bear witness; and in public prayer and administration of the sacraments, I will use only the forms of service which are authorised or allowed by Canon.'

See **Canonical Obedience**.

DECREE (L *decretum*)

RC. A legislative, administrative or judicial PROVISION which supplements or implements the law (e.g. a conciliar decree or a decree of a congregation of the Roman *Curia*). A **general legislative decree**: a legislative decree made by a competent legislator and which is regulated by CANON (c 29: e.g. the decree of a BISHOPS' conference). A **general administrative decree**: a decree which defines more precisely the manner of applying a law or which urges the observance of a law (cc 31–3). A **singular decree**: an administrative ACT whereby a decision is given for a particular case (cc 48–58). A **judicial decree**: a formal pronouncement by a judge which may be procedural or may determine a particular question (c 1617). An **extra-judicial decree**: whenever there are just reasons against the use of a judicial procedure a PENALTY can be imposed by means of an extra-judicial decree (c 1342). This extra-judicial procedure enables, for instance, a diocesan bishop to impose a penalty by means of an administrative decree. See **Constitution**; *Decretum*; **Instruction**; **Precept**; **Rescript**.

C of E. A process by which a lawsuit is commenced in the Court of Arches.

DECRETAL (L *decretalis*)

RC. A papal letter containing a ruling on matters of canonical discipline. The outstanding collection of decretals in Italy and Spain were the *Hadria Collectio* sent by Adrian I to Charlemagne in 774 and the *Hispana Collectio* (sixth century) associated with Isidore of Seville. **False decretals**: the decretals of Pseudo-Isidore assembled in France about 850, and which found their way into later collections; they set out to enhance the position of pope and clergy. The **Decretals of Gregory IX**: the first official collection of papal decretals and CONSTITUTIONS, compiled and published by Raymond of Penafort at the request of Pope Gregory IX. This collection covered the period from the third Lateran Council (1139) and the *Decretum* of Gratian (1141) up to its publication in 1234. It formed part of the *Corpus Iuris Canonici* which remained in force until the 1917 Code. See **Decree**; **Decretalist**; **Decretist**.

DECRETALIST (L *decretalis*)

RC. Commentators on the DECRETALS of the popes writing after Gratian's *Decretum* – e.g. Bernardo di Pavia (*Papiensis*) and Henricius de Segusio (*Hostiensis*). *Papiensis*, an Italian canonist of the twelfth century, wrote the *Summa Decretalium*, the *Summa de Matrimonio*, the *Brevarium Extravagantium* and other works. *Hostiensis*, a CARDINAL, canonist and diplomat of the thirteenth century, wrote the famous *Summa Copiosa*, a synthesis of Roman law and CANON LAW which was in constant use until the seventeenth century. See **Decree**; **Decretal**; **Decretist**.

DECRETIST (L *decretum*, decree)

RC. A commentator on the *Decretum Gratiani*, a canonical treatise which Gratian, a Camaldolese monk teaching at the University of Bologna, produced about 1141. The decretist's work was entitled *Concordia Discordantium Canonum* (harmony of discordant canons), and provided a comprehensive synthesis of the Church's laws. The decretists commented on the *Decretum* by means of GLOSSES or summaries. Notable decretists include Paucapalea, a canonist and possible student of Gratian; Rufinus, an Italian ARCHBISHOP, canonist and theologian who wrote the *Summa Decretorum*, an influential work; Huguccio, Bishop of Ferrara; and a canonist who wrote the *Summa Super Decreta* which was the most complete commentary on Gratian's *Decretum*. See **Decree**; **Decretal**; **Decretalist**; **Gloss**.

DECRETUM (L, decree)

RC. The name given to important writings which brought together the mass of material making up the CANON LAW and set it out in orderly fashion, e.g. the *Decretum* of Burchard of Worms in the eleventh century which was concerned with reorganization of the Church and the maintenance of discipline. This work was soon followed by the *Decretum* of Bishop Ivo of Chartres and the *Sic et Non* of Peter Abelard, a work which influenced Gratian to compile his *Decretum*. Gratian's *Decretum* provided a summary and commentary on the first millennium of Church law. See **Decretalists**; **Decretals**; **Decretist**.

DEDICATION (L *dedicatio*)

RC. The blessing of a particular place such as a CHURCH or a cemetery, usually by the BISHOP (cc 1169, 1205–13). CONSECRATION, on the other hand, is the blessing of certain persons or objects. See **Consecration**.

C of E. This also occurs. In law, it is just a declaration of intent to put aside land for a godly purpose.

DEFECT (L *defectus*)

RC. The absence of an essential factor or element which affects a person who places a juridic ACT. **Defect of legitimate form**: the absence of an element which essentially constitutes a juridic act, as well as the absence of formalities and requisites necessary in law for the act to be valid (c 124 §1). **Defect of consent**: a juridic act which is placed by a person because of irresistible force, grave fear or fraud, ignorance or error, etc. (cc 125, 126). Defect of marital CONSENT is a principal ground for NULLITY of MARRIAGE. A person who lacks sufficient use of reason, or is gravely deficient in discretion of judgement concerning essential matrimonial rights and duties, is incapable of contracting marriage (cc 1095–1103).

DEFENDER OF THE BOND (L *defensor vinculi*)

RC. An official, clerical or lay, appointed in every DIOCESE to defend validity and maintain the sacred bond in cases concerning the NULLITY

of ORDINATION, or the nullity or dissolution of MARRIAGE (c 1432). See
Promoter of Justice.

DELICT (L *delictum*)

RC. The external violation of a law or PRECEPT by a person, which is
seriously imputable to that person on grounds of malice or culpability
(c 1321 §1). The offender is bound by the PENALTY stated in the law or
precept (c 1321 §2). See **Imputability.**

DE MINIMIS (L, concerning trifles)

RC and C of E. Cases which are so minor as not to need formal
authorization in law. For example, in the Church of England,
CONSISTORY COURTS do not, in practice, interfere with the ordinary
annual maintenance of CHURCHES by requesting FACULTIES. See
Consistory Court; Faculty.

DEPOSIT OF FAITH (L *depositio fidei*)

RC. What is 'contained in the word of God, as it has been written or
handed down by tradition; such truths must be believed by divine
and Catholic faith' (c 750). If the Church has not defined a truth
which is contained in Scripture, it is to be believed by 'divine faith'
alone. The SACRAMENTS form part of the 'divine deposit of faith' (c
841). The deposit of faith has been entrusted by Christ to the Church
so that the Church 'by the assistance of the Holy Spirit . . . might
conscientiously guard revealed truth, more intimately penetrate it and
faithfully proclaim and expound it' (c 747 §1). See *Magisterium.*

DEROGATION (L *derogatio*)

RC. A modification or an amendment of a law. If a competent authority
imposes an administrative ACT that conflicts with existing laws,
CUSTOMS or acquired rights, it must add a derogating clause (c 38).
Regulations contained in INSTRUCTIONS (which are intended to make
laws as clear as possible to ensure their observance) do not derogate
from laws. If they conflict with the prescriptions of laws they lose
their force (c 34 §2). See **Abrogation.**

DESUETUDE (L *desuetudo*)

C of E. Disuse. A CUSTOM can fall into disuse, allowing for the
emergence of a new custom: for instance, in *Gore-Booth* v. *Bishop of
Manchester* [1920] 2 KB 412, Lord Coleridge stated *obiter* that
desuetude could be pleaded if a CLERIC (an Anglican cleric) were
accused of illegality in not wearing prescribed vestments in a particular
CHURCH when the wearing of vestments in that church had been

abandoned. An ACT or MEASURE remains in force, even if it has fallen into disuse, until it is repealed. See **Custom**.

DIACONATE (L *diaconatus*, Gk διακονία)

RC. The first grade within the SACRAMENT of ORDERS (c 1009 §1). See **Deacon; Permanent Deacon**.

C of E. One of the three Holy Orders in the Church (canon C1). See **Deacon; Ordinal**.

DICASTERY (L *dicasterium*, Gk δικαστήριον, court of law)

RC. A department of the Roman CURIA. It is usually composed of the Cardinal Prefect (or the presiding ARCHBISHOP), a number of CARDINALS and some BISHOPS, who are aided by a secretary, consultors, senior ADMINISTRATORS and officials (*PB* art. 3 §1). Dicasteries deal with matters submitted to them by the Supreme Pontiff – matters which are reserved to the APOSTOLIC SEE, and also matters beyond the competence of individual bishops or bishops' conferences (*PB* art. 13). See **Appendix III**.

DIOCESAN COURT: see **Consistory Court**.

DIOCESE (L *dioecesis*, Gk διοίκησις)

RC. A PARTICULAR CHURCH being a portion of the Catholic Church which is entrusted to the pastoral care of a BISHOP assisted by PRESBYTERS (c 369). **Territorial diocese**: a diocese is usually limited to a definite territory (c 372 §1). **Personal or non-territorial diocese**: a particular Church set up within a territorially-defined diocese to minister to the needs of the faithful of different rites or for a similar reason, after consultation with the conferences of bishops concerned (c 372 §2). **Metropolitan diocese**: see **Archbishop**. See **Church; Synod**.

C of E. A portion of a PROVINCE under the JURISDICTION of a diocesan bishop (DM ss. 1, 2).

DIONYSIANA

RC. A collection of conciliar CANONS and papal DECRETALS put together at Rome in the early part of the sixth century by Dionysius Exiguus, a Scythian monk. It was the first important attempt to provide the Western Church with a unified system of law. This collection was in use up to the seventh century. An augmented form, the *Dionysio-Hadriana*, was sent by Pope Hadrian I to the emperor Charlemagne in 774. A number of private collections of CANON LAW followed culminating in the twelfth century with the *DECRETUM* of Gratian. See **Decretals;** *Liber Canonum*.

DIRECTORY (L *directorium*)

RC. A document containing general DECREES which apply to different bodies within the Church, e.g. SCDW directory on children's Masses *Pueros Baptizatos* (1973).

DISPARITY OF CULT (L *disparitas cultus*)

RC. An expression used to describe a MARRIAGE which has taken place between a baptized Catholic (or a person received into the Church) and a non-baptized person (c 1086 §1). Disparity of cult is a diriment IMPEDIMENT to marriage, which the local ORDINARY can dispense with only upon certain conditions (c 1125).

DISPENSATION (L *dispensatio*)

RC. An exemption from ECCLESIASTICAL LAW, granted in a particular case and issued by one who enjoys executive power, such as the ORDINARY, or the APOSTOLIC SEE in reserved cases (cc 85–93). The power to dispense is granted by law and can be delegated; examples include the power to dispense from matrimonial IMPEDIMENTS (c 1078) and from the obligations of private VOWS (c 1196). **Dispensation super rato**: dispensation granted by the pope to dissolve a ratified but unconsummated MARRIAGE (cc 1142, 1697–1706). See **Postulation**.

C of E. The power to relax a law in a particular case where its effect would not be beneficial; examples would be the granting of a 'common LICENCE' for a marriage without BANNS by the ordinary in his DIOCESE, and of a 'special licence' by the Archbishop of Canterbury (canon B34; MA s. 5). See **Ordinary**.

THE DIVINE OFFICE (L *Divinum Officium*)

RC. The daily prayer of the Church. PRIESTS and DEACONS aspiring to the PRIESTHOOD are obliged to pray according to proper and approved liturgical books (c 276 §2). The single official version in English is the Liturgy of the Hours (c 1173–5), wherein Lauds and Vespers are considered to be the chief hours (*SC* 89). The fulfilment of the Divine Office by priests ought to be an extension during the different hours of the day of the prayer and thanksgiving offered by them in the celebration of the EUCHARIST (see 'Presbyterorum Ordinis' *AAS* 58 (1966), 991–1024).

DIVORCE AND REMARRIAGE

RC. A ratified and consummated MARRIAGE cannot be dissolved other than by death (c 1141). A marriage may be declared null when it is not a valid marriage, or dissolved when ratified but not consummated.

After the ANNULMENT or dissolution, the parties are free to remarry. See **Indissolubility**; **Nullity**.

C of E. Marriage is defined as a 'union permanent and life-long . . . till death them do part . . . to the exclusion of all others on either side' (canon B30(1)). This definition implicitly prohibits divorce by dissolution and, with it, the remarriage of a party whose marriage has been dissolved. However, a statement was produced by the GENERAL SYNOD in 1981 to the effect that there are circumstances in which a divorced person may remarry in church while his or her former spouse is living. Guidelines were issued by the House of Bishops in 1985 in the light of this statement. They took the view that clergy who believed in the possibility of a second marriage ought to be free in certain circumstances to solemnize such a marriage (House of Bishops' report 'Marriage Discipline', General Synod 669, 13 Feb. 1985). In accordance with the freedom proposed in these guidelines many diocesan BISHOPS have drawn up NORMS to deal with the problem of remarriage. It is common for such norms to require that the bishop be consulted for his advice and guidance and to leave the final decision to the discretion of the minister. See **Marriage**.

DOCTRINE (L *doctrina*)

RC. The teaching of the Church. **Definitive doctrine**: doctrinal statements by the pope and the COLLEGE OF BISHOPS on matters of faith and morals (c 749). The faithful must adhere to this revealed doctrine of the *MAGISTERIUM* of the Church with the assent of faith (c 750). **Non-definitive doctrine**: doctrine created by the pope and the College of Bishops on matters of faith and morals. Such doctrine requires submission, adherence and respect on the part of the faithful, but not an assent of faith (cc 752, 753). Papal encyclicals are a source of non-definitive doctrine; so also are the Vatican II statements of the College of Bishops. See *Obsequium*.

C of E. The doctrine of the Church is 'grounded in the Holy Scriptures, and in such teachings of the ancient Fathers and Councils of the Church as are agreeable to the said Scriptures'(canon A5). It is to be found, particularly, in the Thirty-Nine Articles of Religion, the BCP and the Ordinal. See **Formulary**.

DOMICILE (L *domicilium*)

RC. Residence in a defined territory (cc 372, 518). A person acquires domicile in the territory of a PARISH or a DIOCESE if he or she intends to remain there permanently or has lived there for five years; such a person is called an *INCOLA* (c 102 §1). **Quasi-domicile**: a person acquires quasi-domicile if he or she intends to remain for a period of three months or has lived in the territory for three months; such a person is called an *ADVENA* (c 102 §2). Domicile or quasi-domicile is not always 'voluntary' but may be 'necessary', i.e. acquired solely by means of a PROVISION of law. Such is the case with members of religious institutes and of SOCIETIES OF APOSTOLIC LIFE (cc 103, 105). See *Peregrinus*; *Vagus*.

DOUBT OF FACT (L *dubium facti*)

RC. A state of uncertainty whether or not a given fact envisaged by the law is clearly demonstrated, e.g. a doubt over the fact of BAPTISM in a particular case. A DISPENSATION can be granted by the ORDINARY for a doubt of fact.

DOUBT OF LAW (L *dubium legis*)

RC. A state of uncertainty as to the existence or meaning of a law. Such uncertainty can also pertain to a vital element in the effectiveness of a law, e.g. its lawful PROMULGATION. A doubtful law is not binding (c 14).

DUPLEX QUERELA (L, double complaint)

C of E. A form of action whereby a CLERIC can sue a BISHOP for refusing to institute him or her to a BENEFICE after PRESENTATION. The suit is normally heard in an appellate tribunal which comprises the ARCHBISHOP of the PROVINCE, and the DEAN OF THE ARCHES, or AUDITOR. The corresponding action of the patron (called *quare impedit*) is brought in the temporal court. See **Court of Ecclesiastical Causes Reserved**.

E

EASEMENT

    RC. A right attached to a piece of land which entitles the owner to exercise some right over adjacent land in different ownership; common examples are a right of way and a right to light. An easement is seen as an example of the ALIENATION of the property rights of the Church limiting its *dominium* or ownership (c 1291). Alienation of Church property only occurs where the COMMON LAW structure prevails. In countries which follow the civil law tradition, ownership involves possession of property in the full sense (c 1256).

    C of E. An easement may be created over a CHURCHYARD (*Re St Martin Le Grand, York* [1989] 2 All ER 711). A legal easement may be granted over unconsecrated land (*Re St Peter's, Bushey Heath* [1971] 1 WLR 357). A right of way or other easement over the land of a redundant CHURCH which does not vest in the Diocesan Board of Finance may be granted by the Church Commissioners, where deemed necessary, to a Redundant Churches Fund, or another body in whom the site vests (PM s. 60(1)). Where such a right was previously enjoyed by churchgoers it may continue to be exercised for the purpose of visiting the church and for the body in whom the right vests to perform its functions (PM s. 60(2)).

EASTER OFFERING

    C of E. An allocation of ALMS to the INCUMBENT by reason of his or her office. Historically, parishioners were directed to pay their parson, VICAR or CURATE (or their deputies) ecclesiastical dues as well as to make an offering at Easter (Tithes and Offerings Act, 1548 §10). The incumbent is obliged to declare the amount of the Easter Offering received for income tax purposes.

EASTERN CATHOLIC CHURCHES (L *Orientales Ecclesiae*)

    RC. Eastern Churches (formerly known as 'Uniate Churches') which are in communion with the APOSTOLIC SEE but which have their own LITURGY, ecclesiastical discipline and patriarchates (with the exception of the Maronite Church).

ECCLESIASTICAL LAW (L *lex ecclesiastica*)

    In the strict sense, law made for the Church by the state, in contrast with CANON LAW (which in this sense is law made by the Church for itself).

RC. The internal law of the Church (John Paul II: *Sacrae Disciplinae Leges* (1983: issued on the PROMULGATION of *CIC* 'De legibus ecclesiasticis'). This term is sometimes used interchangeably with 'canon law'.

C of E. Law which has been created for the Church by the state. T. G. Watkin suggests that 'ecclesiastical law made by the State for the Church of England therefore encompasses the canon law as well' ('Vestiges of Establishment – The Ecclesiastical and Canon Law of the Church in Wales', *ELJ* 2 (1990), 110 at 111). Ecclesiastical law has been defined as 'the law relating to any matter concerning the Church of England administered and enforced in any court' (*HLE* par. 301; *AG* v. *Dean and Chapter of Ripon Cathedral* [1945] Ch 239 at 245 per Uthwatt J). Furthermore, ecclesiastical law has been described as 'part of the general law of England – of the common law – in the wider sense' (*MacKonochie* v. *Lord Penzance* (1881) 6 AppCas 424 at 446 per Lord Blackburn; *Kirkham* v. *Chief Constable of Manchester* [1990] 2 QB 283 at 292 per Lloyd LJ). In this sense it is deduced from various sources including ancient canon law and CUSTOM as well as from present CANONS and MEASURES passed by Parliament (*Kemp* v. *Wickes* (1809) 3 Phillimore 264 at 276 per Sir John Nicholl). See **Canon Law**; **Common Law**.

ECUMENICAL COUNCIL (L *concilium oecumenicum*)

RC. A solemn assembly of the COLLEGE OF BISHOPS (e.g. the Second Vatican Council, 1962–5) which, united with the pope as its head, exercises supreme power over the whole Church. It decides upon matters of DOCTRINE and discipline (cc 337–41). See *Magisterium*.

ECUMENISM (L *oecumenicus*, Gk οἰκουμενικός)

RC. The fostering of relations with other Churches. A diocesan BISHOP is to act charitably towards persons who are not in full communion with the Catholic Church and is to foster ecumenism as the Church understands it (c 383 §3). Catholics are to participate in the ecumenical movement, the purpose of which is the restoration of Christian unity (c 755). In cases of NECESSITY or of 'genuine spiritual advantage' and where it is impossible for the faithful to approach a Catholic minister, they may 'receive the sacraments of penance, Eucharist and anointing of the sick from non-Catholic ministers in whose Churches these sacraments are valid' (c 844 §2); Christians not in full communion with the Church who are in a state of grave necessity may receive the SACRAMENTS under certain conditions (c 844 §4). A PRESBYTER may celebrate the EUCHARIST in the edifice of another Church for a just cause and with the express permission of the bishop (c 933; Vatican

II decree on ecumenism '*Unitatis Redintegratio*' (1964)). See **Ecumenical Council.**

C of E. Ministers from other Churches and also their lay members who are baptized and in good standing may participate in Anglican services at the invitation of the INCUMBENT and with the approval of the bishop and/or the PAROCHIAL CHURCH COUNCIL (canon B43(1)). Clergy and lay members of the Church may participate in services at other Churches, subject to certain approvals and restrictions (canon B43(2), (3), (6)). The incumbent of a PARISH may, with the approval of the bishop and the PCC, invite members of another Church to participate in joint worship with his own congregation, or to use a CHURCH building in the parish for their own form of worship (canon B43(9)). A Local Ecumenical Project (or LEP) is a formal agreement between a bishop and the authorities of participating Churches with regard to a parish or part of a parish (canon B44(1)); such an agreement is for a period of up to seven years. See **Intercommunion**; **Lambeth Quadrilateral.**

ELECTION (L *electio*, choice)

RC. A means whereby the PROVISION of an office in the Church is effected (c 147). Simple election and acceptance by the one elected usually confers office. However, confirmation of a prior election by a competent authority may be required for the conferral of office, e.g. the election of a superior of a religious institute or the election of a BISHOP by a CATHEDRAL CHAPTER which has the right of election. General NORMS set out in *CIC* apply to canonical elections (i.e. of an individual to an office: cc 164–79). However, particular norms apply to the election of the ROMAN PONTIFF (c 332; see also the apostolic constitution *Universi Dominici Gregis* (John Paul II, 1996). See **Provision.**

C of E. **Elections to the General Synod**: membership of the Upper House of the CONVOCATION in each PROVINCE is made up of the ARCHBISHOP and the diocesan bishops, along with six elected members in Canterbury (three in York). Membership of the Lower Houses of the Convocations is made up of a number of selected PROCTORS (i.e. clergy representatives), not exceeding 170 for Canterbury or eighty for York. However, most of the clergy representatives are directly elected, with each DIOCESE having three elected clergy representatives (Sodor and Man and Europe have one and two respectively). Membership of the House of Laity is governed by the CRR (part V). It is mostly made up of persons elected by diocesan electors. **Elections to the Diocesan Synods**: members, clerical and lay, are elected from the deanery SYNODS in the dioceses every three years (CRR r. 32). **Elections to the Deanery Synods**: membership of the deanery synods includes the clergy in the deaneries, along with lay representatives (CRR r. 24). Parochial representatives are elected by the annual parochial CHURCH meetings every three years (CRR r. 25). See **General Synod**; **Parochial Church Council**; **Synod**.

ELECTORAL ROLL

C of E. A list of persons who are qualified to vote in the PARISH on the PAROCHIAL CHURCH COUNCIL, and/or at the parish annual general meeting. Such a list has to be maintained in every parish. Those whose names appear on the roll must be at least sixteen years of age, baptized and members of the C of E or of CHURCHES in communion with the C of E. They must also be resident in the parish or have habitually attended public worship in the parish for over six months before enrolment and have also signed the application form (CRR r. 1(2)). The PCC has a duty to keep the roll up to date. The roll must be reviewed annually and a new roll compiled every sixth year after 1990. (CRR r. 2). A CLERIC's name may not appear on the roll.

EMBER DAYS

RC. Ember days were replaced in 1969 by days of prayer for various needs. See **Fasting and Abstinence**; **Rogation Days**.

C of E. According to BCP, the Wednesday, Friday and Saturday after the first Sunday in Lent, Whitsunday, 14 September and 13 December. These days are to be kept as days of FASTING AND ABSTINENCE. Also, they fall before times of ORDINATION to the sacred ministry when special prayers are said, which is why ASB has additional ember days before the Feast of St Peter (29 June) and the Feast of St Michael and All Angels (29 September). The diocesan BISHOP may direct that certain days be also kept as ember days. See **Fasting and Abstinence**; **Feast Day**; **Rogation Days**.

ENCLOSURE: SEE **Cloister.**

ENROLMENT (L *ascriptio*)

EC. The term used in *CCEO* for the INCARDINATION of a CLERIC (*CCEO* c 357). Enrolment in an EPARCHY only ceases by valid enrolment into another eparchy or by loss of the clerical state (*CCEO* c 364).

EPARCHY (L *eparchia*, Gk ἐπαρχία)

EC. A DIOCESE. A portion of God's people which is entrusted to the pastoral care of the BISHOP with the cooperation of the PRESBYTERATE, which constitutes a particular Church within the one, holy, catholic and apostolic Church (*CCEO* c 177 §1). It may be erected, modified or suppressed within the boundaries of a PATRIARCHAL CHURCH by the patriarch with the consent of the SYNOD OF BISHOPS of the patriarchal Church after he has consulted with the APOSTOLIC SEE, for a serious reason; in other cases such action is solely within the competence of the Apostolic See (*CCEO* cc 85 §1; 177 §2). The eparchial bishop governs the eparchy in his own name and exercises proper ordinary and immediate power as a VICAR and LEGATE of Christ. His exercise of power is ultimately regulated by the supreme authority of the Church (*CCEO* c 178). A bishop to whom an eparchy has not been entrusted for governing in his own name is called a **titular bishop** (*CCEO* c 179). See **Exarchy**; **Patriarchal Church**.

EPISCOPATE (L *episcopatus,* the office and dignity of a BISHOP, episcopate; Gk ἐπίσκοπος, overseer)

 RC. One of the three grades within the SACRAMENT OF ORDERS, after the DIACONATE and the PRESBYTERATE (c 1009 §1; c 1008). See **Bishop**.

 C of E. One of the three Holy Orders in the Church (canon C1). See **Bishop**; **Ordinal**.

EQUITY (L *aequitas*, fairness)

 RC. The application of a standard which seems just and right in a particular circumstance where the rule of law seems unreasonable or unfair. Equity considers the spirit of the law rather than the letter of the law – it looks at the intention rather than the action. It is based on Aristotle's concept of *epieikia*, and is a hallmark of the civil law tradition. **Canonical equity**: a general relaxation of the law allowed in the following circumstances: (i) in non-penal matters where the law is silent and there is a gap or *lacuna* in the law (c19); (ii) to produce a just result where the law requires the opposite result; (iii) to temper the law with a notion of mercy, where allowed (i.e. the faithful have a right to be judged with equity (c 221 §2); (iv) where executive actions taken by judges or ADMINISTRATORS grant DISPENSATIONS (cc 85, 87, 89, 1196, 1197).

ERROR OF PERSON (L *error personae*)

 RC. An error concerning the identity of a person. Such an error invalidates a MARRIAGE (c 1097 §1).

 C of E. The position is the same.

ERROR OF QUALITY (L *error qualitatis*)

 RC. An error concerning the 'quality' of a person, e.g. his or her professional or financial status. Such an error does not normally invalidate a Marriage unless the quality was 'directly and principally intended' (c 1097 §2). See **Error of Person**.

C of E. The same view is held.

Eucharist (L *eucharistia*, Gk εὐχαριστία, thanksgiving)

> *RC.* The Sacrament of the Lord's own body and blood, instituted by Christ at the Last Supper. The Character of the Eucharist is sacrifice, communion and presence (John Paul II: encyclical letter *Redemptor Hominis* (1979), 20). It is 'the summit and source of all Christian worship and life'; it is not only a memorial of Christ's death and resurrection, but is also a sacrifice 'in which the sacrifice of the cross is perpetuated' (c 897). In the Eucharist (or Mass, as it is often called) 'Christ offers himself substantially present under the appearance of bread and wine to God the Father, and gives himself as spiritual nourishment to the faithful who are associated with him in his offering' (c 899). A Priest may offer Mass for the living or the dead (c 901). See **Excommunication**; **Feast of Obligation**; **Last Rites**.

> *C of E.* 'The Holy Sacrament of the Lord's Supper' instituted by Christ (canon B12; Thirty-Nine Articles of Religion, nos. 25, 28). It is: 'the continual remembrance of the sacrifice of the death of Christ, and of the benefits which we receive thereby'; its benefits are 'the strengthening and refreshing of our souls by the Body and Blood of Christ' (BCP Catechism). It is also known as Holy Communion. See **Feast Day**.

Evangelical Counsels (L *consilia evangelica*)

> *RC.* The generic term for the Vows of poverty, chastity and obedience professed by members of religious and secular institutes and by those called to the eremitic life (cc 573–6). They are based upon the teaching and example of Christ (*LG* 43).

Exarchy (L *exarchia*, Gk ἔξαρχος)

> *EC.* A portion of God's people committed to an exarch which owing to special circumstances is not erected as an Eparchy and which is established within territorial or other limits (*CCEO* c 311 §1). An exarchy can be established inside but is more often established outside the territorial limits of a patriarchate. The patriarch can with the consent of the permanent Synod erect, modify or suppress exarchies (*CCEO* 85 §3). The establishment, modification and suppression of exarchies outside the territorial boundaries of a Patriarchal Church belongs to the Apostolic See (*CCEO* c 311 §2). The exarch governs the exarchy in his own name or in the name of the one who appointed him (*CCEO* c 312). The law applying to eparchies also applies to exarchies unless there are Provisions and evidence to the contrary (*CCEO* c 313).

EXCARDINATION (L *excardinatio*)

RC. A juridical ACT whereby a CLERIC is no longer INCARDINATED in one PARTICULAR CHURCH. It occurs when a cleric transfers to another particular church in which case written permission must be granted by the BISHOP of the DIOCESE he is leaving (a letter of excardination) as well as of the diocese he is entering (a letter of incardination) (cc 267, 268–72). See *Exeat*; **Incardination**.

EXCEPTION (L *exceptio*)

RC. A subordinate issue in the form of a claim or complaint brought by the defendant, which has to be settled before a court can settle the principal issue before it. **Dilatory exception**: a claim or complaint which in some way modifies the procedure of the court. A dilatory exception can range from a minor procedural point to a major procedural DEFECT (c 1459). **Peremptory exception**: a claim or complaint which quashes the suit. A peremptory exception might claim that the case has already been settled by another court (such a claim must be lodged before the joinder of issues) or that the matter should not be heard (cc 1462, 1491–1500). See *Res Iudicata*; *Restitutio in Integrum*; *Transactio*.

EXCLAUSTRATION (L *exclaustratio*)

RC. Authorization granted to a member of a religious institute professed of perpetual VOWS to leave the institute for a period of up to three years. The supreme moderator grants an INDULT of exclaustration. He does so with the consent of the local ORDINARY, if the professed member is a CLERIC. An indult is only granted for a grave reason, e.g. a vocational crisis. Enforced exclaustration is imposed by the APOSTOLIC SEE upon a professed member for disciplinary reasons. Exclaustration frees a member of a religious institute from the obligations of religious life, e.g. living in community, but he remains subject to the care of his superior and the local ordinary (cc 686–7). See **Indult**.

EXCOMMUNICATION (L *excommunicatio*)

RC. A CENSURE whereby a person is excluded from the communion of the faithful and barred from certain aspects of the public life of the Church. Such a person cannot celebrate or receive the SACRAMENTS or have any ministerial participation in any ceremonial of public worship, or discharge any ecclesiastical office, ministry or function (c 1331). It is the gravest of the Church's three medicinal PENALTIES. An automatic (*LATAE SENTENTIAE*) excommunication is incurred by an apostate from the faith, a heretic or a schismatic (c 1364). See **Apostasy**; **Censure**; **Heresy**; **Interdict**; **Schism**; **Suspension**.

C of E. A spiritual censure for certain grave offences such as impugning
the CONSTITUTION or rites and ceremonies of the Church (see *The
Canons Ecclesiastical*, 1603). The offence has become obsolete.
However, canon B14 deals with 'notorious offenders not to be admitted
to Holy Communion'. The canon applies when the minister is
persuaded that 'anyone of his cure' is in 'malicious and open contention with his neighbours' or has committed 'other grave and open
sin'. The minister is under a duty to report the matter to the diocesan
BISHOP and to obey his direction (*R* v. *Dibdin* [1910] P 57 at 137). If
the bishop bars the person from Holy Communion the minister
must first 'call' the person who shall be 'advertised . . . that in any
wise he presume not to come to the Lord's Table'. Furthermore, under
the CANON, if the minister is satisfied that admission will cause 'a
grave and immediate scandal to the congregation' the minister has a
duty not to admit. The ORDINARY must be informed within seven days
of the exclusion. The ordinary is to afford the person an opportunity
for review.

EXEAT (L, let him depart)

    RC. A letter of EXCARDINATION.

EXEMPTION (L *exemptio*, taking out)

    RC. A DISPENSATION from accountability to others. For example, minors
are subject to the authority of parents or guardians as to the exercise of
their rights except in those areas where they are exempted by divine or
CANON LAW (c 98 §2). **Exempt diocese**: a DIOCESE which is directly
subject to the APOSTOLIC SEE and which is exempt from the authority of
a metropolitan of a PROVINCE (e.g. the dioceses of Switzerland: c 431
§2). **Exempt institute**: an INSTITUTE OF CONSECRATED LIFE which the
pope has exempted from the JURISDICTION of the local ORDINARY in order
to better provide for the good of the institute and the needs of the
apostolate. The pope may place the institute under his own jurisdiction
or that of another ecclesiastical authority (c 591; see also *LG* 45; *CD*
35). Each institute has a right to its own autonomy of life (especially
with regard to governance) which the local ordinary is obliged to
safe-guard and protect (c 586 §§1, 2). **Exemption of clerics or
religious**: in certain countries CLERICS or religious are exempted from
civic duties such as military service. In such circumstances, clerics
and candidates for ORDINATION should not volunteer for military
service without the permission of the local ordinary (c 289). **Exempt
documents**: documents which no one is obliged to exhibit if they
cannot be communicated without risk of harm or without violating the
obligation to observe secrecy (e.g. the issuing of affidavits: c 1546).
See **Immunity**.

EX INTEGRO (L)

RC. In entirety. Areas of law which have been entirely reorganized.

EXORCISM (L *exorcismus*)

RC. The removing of evil from a person, place, etc. through invocation
of the Blessed Trinity. It is one of the SACRAMENTALS of the Church.
Only a priest 'endowed with pity, knowledge, prudence and integrity
of life' may exorcize a person who is 'possessed'. 'Special and express'
permission for him to do so has to be granted by the local ORDINARY (c
1172 §§1, 2). See **Sacramentals**.

C of E. Only an experienced person authorized by the diocesan BISHOP
is permitted to carry out an exorcism. Continuing pastoral care is to
follow the exorcizing of a person (Archbishop of Canterbury: *Statement to the General Synod*, 30 June 1975).

EXPEDITISSIME (L)

RC and EC. Most expeditiously. A judge is required to make special
judicial decisions without delay; there is no appeal over these decisions
(c 1629; *CCEO* c 1310).

EXPIATORY (L *expiatorius*, atoning)

RC. An expiatory PENALTY: a penal sanction under the law aimed at
punishing an offender for the damage caused to society by an offence
while at the same time deterring others from behaving in a similar
way. Expiatory penalties include: a prohibition or order concerning
residency and deprivation of power, office, function, right, etc. (c 1336).
The remission of an expiatory penalty, unlike that of a CENSURE, is not
automatic upon the cessation of the offender's CONTUMACY but may
be inflicted indefinitely.

EXTRAORDINARY FORM (L *forma extraordinaria*)

RC. A MARRIAGE celebrated before two witnesses but without the active
assistance of a PRESBYTER, or of a DEACON who has the FACULTY to
assist at marriage in a situation where a qualified presbyter or deacon
is absent for a month (c 1116). See **Canonical Form**; **Sacramental
Form**.

EXTRAORDINARY MINISTER (L *minister extraordinarius*)

RC. A minister of a SACRAMENT or other liturgical rite who functions
when there is an insufficient number of ORDINARY ministers to fulfil
pastoral needs (c 230 §3). Where LECTORS and ACOLYTES are few, other
lay persons can carry out their functions of, for example, exercising
the ministry of the word or distributing Holy Communion.

F

FACULTY (L *facultas*)

RC. A delegated power of governance granted by law or a competent authority. A diocesan BISHOP is granted a habitual faculty by the APOSTOLIC SEE. PRESBYTERS and DEACONS are granted the faculty of PREACHING (c 764). A confessor is granted a faculty to exercise the power of ABSOLUTION (c 966).

C of E. A LICENCE granted by the diocesan CHANCELLOR in the CONSISTORY COURT allowing alterations to be carried out to a CHURCH building, its contents or the CHURCHYARD (FJM ss. 1, 3, 4, 6, 7, 8; FJR ss. 11, 15, 16).

FASTING AND ABSTINENCE (L *ieiunium et abstinentia*)

RC. Forms of penance which the Christian community is obliged by divine law to undertake (c 1249). Abstinence from meat (or some other food which the BISHOPS' conference can determine) is to be observed on all Fridays (unless a solemnity falls on a Friday); this requirement can be qualified by the active practice of some other work. On Ash Wednesday and Good Friday both abstinence and fasting are to be observed (c 1251). All who are over fourteen years of age are bound for life by the law of abstinence. All who have attained their majority are bound by the law of fasting until they reach the age of sixty (c 1252).

C of E. BCP sets out a list of days of fasting or abstinence to be observed in the year. The list comprises: (i) the forty days of Lent; (ii) the Ember Days at the four seasons (the Wednesday, Friday and Saturday after the first Sunday in Lent, the Feast of Pentecost, 14 September and 13 December); (iii) the three Rogation Days (the Monday, Tuesday and Wednesday before Ascension Day); (iv) all Fridays, except Christmas Day. Lent is mentioned as a time for special observance, particularly Ash Wednesday and Holy Week (canon B6(3)). Days of discipline and self denial in the ASB include all Fridays except those falling on Christmas Day, the Epiphany, or on any festival or major holy day outside Lent, and also excepting the Fridays after Christmas Day and Easter Day (ASB 22). The new Calendar excludes principal feasts and festivals outside Lent, and Fridays from Easter Day to Pentecost. Eves of principal feasts, however, are included as days of discipline and self denial (CYCLC 13). See **Ember Days**, **Rogation Days**.

FATALIA LEGIS (L, things decreed by law)

RC. Time limits set by the law, peremptory legal deadlines. Such deadlines cannot be extended nor validly shortened without the parties' consent (c 1465): e.g. a PETITIONER has ten days to appeal against the rejection of a petition; after such time the right is extinguished (c 1505 §4). As a rule legal deadlines which refer to the court and not to the parties are non-peremptory. See *Libellus*.

FAVOUR OF THE LAW (L *favor iuris*)

RC. Usually, where there is doubt in the mind of a judge over the moral certitude of a matter to be determined by SENTENCE he must pronounce that the right of the PETITIONER has not been established and must dismiss the RESPONDENT as absolved. However, by EXCEPTION, if the petition is one which enjoys the favour of the law, the judge must determine in favour of it (c 1608 §4). For example, the validity of MARRIAGE enjoys the favour of the law (c 1060) in the absence of moral certitude – but if there is a doubtful privilege of the faith (e.g. one of the parties is doubtfully baptized) the freedom to remarry must be recognized. See **Pauline Privilege**; **Petrine Privilege**.

FEAST DAY (L *festum*)

A day on which important events in the life of the Lord Jesus Christ or of the SAINTS are commemorated. Feast days are classified under three main headings: Sundays; movable feasts, the most important of which are Easter and Whitsunday; immovable feasts, in particular Christmas and Epiphany.

RC. In the Church calendar festivals are of lesser importance than solemnities, but of greater importance than memorials.

C of E. In the Anglican calendar greater feasts are known as 'RED-LETTER DAYS' and have their own collect and readings in the EUCHARIST and offices, as do festivals in the RC calendar. Holy Communion is to be celebrated in every PARISH CHURCH on Sundays and on other principal feast days, Ash Wednesday and Maundy Thursday (canon B14). The principal feast days of special observance are Christmas Day, Epiphany, the Annunciation of the Blessed Virgin Mary, Easter Day, Ascension Day, Whitsunday or Pentecost, Trinity Sunday and All Saints' Day (canon B6(2)). See **Feast of Obligation**; **Red-Letter Days**; **Appendix I**.

FEAST OF OBLIGATION

RC. An important FEAST DAY, or a Sunday, upon which the Christian faithful are bound to participate in the Mass (c 1247). These holy days of obligation are Christmas, the Epiphany, the Ascension, Corpus Christi, Holy Mary Mother of God, the Immaculate Conception, the Assumption, St Joseph, the apostles Peter and Paul and All Saints (c 1246 §1). However, the observance of these feasts, apart from Sundays, varies somewhat from country to country. In England and Wales the holy days of obligation are Christmas, the Epiphany, the Ascension, Corpus Christi, SS Peter and Paul, the Assumption of the Blessed Virgin Mary and All Saints. The Christian faithful are bound to receive Communion only once a year, and this Precept has to be fulfilled during the Easter season (c 920 §§1, 2).

C of E. According to the BCP Rubric, every confirmed parishioner has a duty to communicate at least three times in the year, of which Easter shall be one. Canon B15 requires those confirmed to receive Holy Communion regularly, and especially at the festivals of Christmas, Easter and Whitsun.

Ferendae Sententiae (L, declaration of judgement)

RC. A Penalty which is inflicted by a decision which is binding only after it has been imposed (c 1314). See **Censure**; *Latae sententiae*; **Penalty**.

First Fruits and Tenths (L *primitiae et decimae*)

C of E. Payments originally made to the pope which were appropriated by the Crown at the Reformation. They were introduced by Pandulph, the papal Legate during the reigns of King John (1199–1216) and King Henry III (1216–72). **First Fruits** (also called *primitiae* or *annatis*): the first year's whole profits of a spiritual preferment. *Tenths* (or *decimae*): the tenth part of the annual profit of each living. These payments were extinguished under The First Fruits and Tenths Measure, 1926. See **Queen Anne's Bounty**.

Font (L *fons*)

RC. A baptismal font must be provided in every Parish Church (c 858 §1). By exception, Baptism may be celebrated in the sanctuary and from a small bowl or vessel. Furthermore, baptism may be celebrated outside the parish church: a font may be erected in a secondary church or Oratory in the parish when the Bishop so determines (c 858 §2).

C of E. A font must be provided in every church for the purpose of administering Holy Baptism (canon F1(1)). The Parochial Church Council is obliged to provide and maintain the font (canon F14). The normal position of the font is near the main entrance to the church; however, the bishop may determine otherwise. See **Baptism**.

FORMULARY

C of E. The historic formularies of the Church as contained in the Thirty-Nine Articles of Religion, BCP and the Ordinal, to which ministers and those about to be ordained are obliged to make a DECLARATION OF ASSENT (canon C15). (See also 'Examination for Holy Orders' (canon C7)). These formularies are the 'title deeds' of the Church.

FORUM (L)

RC. A tribunal. For **competent forum** (e.g. the ROMAN PONTIFF, the Roman Rota, judges, etc.) see cc 1404–16. **External forum**: this deals with matters which are likely to have juridical or social effects, e.g. the power of governance (c 130). **Internal forum**: this deals with sacramental matters, i.e. matters concerning the SACRAMENT of penance. It also deals with non-sacramental matters, i.e. matters concerning the giving of advice on issues of conscience, e.g. a DISPENSATION from an OCCULT IMPEDIMENT (i.e. one that cannot be proved in an external forum) to MARRIAGE. A dispensation from the external forum is unnecessary if the impediment later becomes public (c 1082). If a dispensation granted for the internal sacramental forum later becomes public, a new dispensation is required from the external forum. See **Impediment, Occult.**

FREEHOLD

C of E. The nature of an INCUMBENT's interest in the PARISH and CHURCHYARD. His or her rights of ownership are subject to certain limitations (see **Faculty**). See also **Benefice; Churchwarden; Induction; Institution.**

G

GENERAL SYNOD (L *synodus*, Gk σύνοδος, assembly)

C of E. The supreme body within the Church's structure of internal governance. It is made up of the House of Bishops, the House of Clergy and the House of Laity. It must appoint a legislative committee. A Standing Committee may be appointed and such others as the General Synod deems expedient. The functions of the General Synod are both legislative and deliberative: to pass legislation on Church matters by means of MEASURE, CANON, order or Act of Synod (SGM s. 2(1) and sched. 2, at 6); to deliberate on public issues that are of religious significance. It lacks both a judicial and an executive function. The General Synod's administrative work is carried out by a group of 'subordinate bodies' which both advise the Synod and implement ecclesiastical legislation and synodical policy; examples include the Advisory Board of Ministry, the Board of Social Responsibility, the Doctrine Commission, and the Crown Appointments Commission. Acts of synod have no statutory force, only moral force – the same is true of acts of CONVOCATIONS and also statements by the House of Bishops.

GLEBE (L *glaeba*, soil)

C of E. Any land or tenement which forms part of the emoluments of a BENEFICE. The parsonage house and grounds, however, are not considered as glebe. All glebe land is now vested in and managed by the DIOCESE (Endowments and Glebe Measure, 1976). See **Benefice.**

GLOSS (L *glossa*)

RC. Initially, a brief commentary or explanatory note upon difficult words of a text, usually written in the margin of a manuscript or old edition. The single-word gloss was usually interlined and initialled or given a mark of identification in the margin. This method of interpretation was first applied to legal texts by the jurists who revived the study of Roman law at Bologna in the eleventh century. It was adopted by the canonists and soon developed into a lengthy interpretation of a whole text or of a principle of law contained therein (e.g. the *Glossa Ordinaria* of Accursius). See **Decretalist**; **Decretist**; **Glossator.**

GLOSSATOR (see above)

RC. A medieval legal scholar who composed GLOSSES, the most famous being Irnerius and Accursius. Irnerius was the founder of the school of glossators; Accursius produced an elaborate gloss, the *Glossa Ordinaria*, which after the publication of Gratian's *Decretum* was adopted by later canonists as a method of glossing. The glossators flourished between 1050 and 1250. See **Decretalist**; **Decretist**; **Gloss**.

GRADUS IUDICII (L, stage in a lawsuit)

    RC. An INSTANCE of a certain level of adjudication in the prosecution of a lawsuit.

GRAVE SIN (L *grave peccatum*)

    RC. A serious sin. All grave sins (or 'mortal' sins as they used to be called) committed after BAPTISM must be confessed in individual CONFESSION (c 988 §1). See **Venial Sin**.

GUILD CHURCH

    C of E. One of sixteen CHURCHES within the City of London which have their own INCUMBENTS (called 'guild vicars'), guild clerks, CHURCHWARDENS and ELECTORAL ROLLS. The 'guild vicar' is appointed through the patron and the BISHOP for a term of years. Such a church has no PARISH of its own; however, its 'guild vicar' is independent of the incumbent of the territorial parish wherein it lies. The guild churches established under the City of London (Guild Churches) Act 1952 (s. 4(1) sched. 1) are the following: All Hallows London Wall, St Andrew's Holborn, St Benet Paul's Wharf, St Botolph without Aldersgate, St Dunstan in the West, St Ethelburga Bishopsgate, St Katherine's Cree, St Lawrence Jewry, St Margaret Pattens, St Martin Ludgate, St Mary Abchurch, St Mary Aldermanbury, St Mary Aldermary, St Mary Woolnoth, St Michael Paternoster Royal and St Nicholas Cole Abbey. They remain within the DIOCESE of London and the relevant deanery or archdeaconry. These churches provide, in particular, for the spiritual needs of those who work in the City during the week. See **Patronage**.

H

HERESY (L *haeresis*, Gk αἵρεσις)

RC. The obstinate denial of a truth which must be believed with divine and Catholic faith, or an obstinate doubting of the same truth (c 751). The Christian faithful are bound to believe with divine and Catholic faith a truth contained in Scripture or Tradition, i.e. what is part of the DEPOSIT OF FAITH and is proposed as divinely revealed by the Church's MAGISTERIUM (c 750). A heretic incurs EXCOMMUNICATION *LATAE SENTENTIAE* and, if a CLERIC, he can also incur various expiatory PENALTIES (cc 1364, 1336). See **Abjuration; Apostasy; Schism**.

C of E. The holding of a false opinion which is repugnant to Christian DOCTRINE clearly revealed in Scripture (*Burn's Ecclesiastical Law* (14th edn.), vol. 2, pp. 304, 305). The doctrine of the Church is 'grounded in Holy Scripture and in such teaching of the ancient Fathers and Councils of the Church as are agreeable to the said Scriptures' (canon A5). No statutory definition of heresy has existed since the repeal of the Act of Supremacy, 1558. However, a cleric can still be charged with heresy provided that the obnoxious opinions and the exact terms in which they were uttered or published are distinctly stated (*Williams* v. *Bishop of Salisbury* (1864), 2 Moore PCCNS 375 at 423). Heresy is not an offence on the part of a lay person.

HIERARCH (L *archiereus*, Gk ἀρχιερεύς)

EC. The local ORDINARY according to the NORM of law, e.g. the eparchial or the exarchial BISHOP (*CCEO* c 178), or the superior general, etc. of an ORDER or a religious congregation (*CCEO* c 515. **Assembly of hierarchs**: an assembly of patriarchs, metropolitans, eparchial bishops (and sometimes local hierarchs of CHURCHES *SUI IURIS*) convened by the patriarch or another authority designated by the APOSTOLIC SEE; it meets to foster unity of action, to promote the good of religion and to preserve ecclesiastical discipline (*CCEO* c 322 §1). See **Eparchy; Exarchy**.

HOLY SEE: see **Apostolic See**.

HOMILY (L *homilia*)

RC. A pre-eminent form of PREACHING by which a sacred text is expounded; it is part of the LITURGY and is reserved to a PRESBYTER or DEACON (c 767 §1). A homily is to be given at all Sunday Masses and Masses on holy days of obligation unless there is a serious reason for its omission (c 767 §2).

C of E. A Sermon is to be preached at least once each Sunday in every Parish (canon B18(1)). A minister, deaconess or licensed lay reader or Lay Worker may preach the sermon; furthermore, a beneficed Cleric may invite any other person to preach, with the Bishop's permission (canon B18(2)). The preacher is to endeavour to glorify God and edify the people through his or her preaching (canon B18(3)).

I

IMMUNITY (L *immunitas*)

RC. A right of freedom from accountability. For example, papal LEGATES such as NUNCIOS have diplomatic immunity from civil power. An EXEMPTION, by contrast, is a DISPENSATION and not a right. See **Legate**.

IMPEDIMENT (L *impedimentum*)

RC. A circumstance or condition which makes an action invalid. **Diriment impediment**: an impediment which renders a person incapable of contracting MARRIAGE validly (c 1073). Impediments of this kind include lack of age, absence of CONSENT, force or fear, and being in holy ORDERS. **Impediment of order**: an obstacle which prevents a person from receiving orders (c 1042); a perpetual impediment is called an irregularity. **Impediment of religion**: a requirement relating to the validity of a temporary profession (e.g. the absence of force, grave fear or fraud) (c 656). **Public impediment**: an impediment which can be proven in the external FORUM (e.g. a prior bond of marriage: c 1074); **Occult impediment**: an impediment based upon circumstances commonly known but which cannot be proven by ecclesiastical or civil documents (e.g. an abduction: c 1074). **Dispensation from an impediment**: since an impediment has the binding force of law, it can only be dispensed by a competent ecclesiastical authority. The local ORDINARY can grant DISPENSATION from all the impediments of ECCLESIASTICAL LAW with the exception of impediments whose dispensation is reserved to the APOSTOLIC SEE (c 1078 §1). The Apostolic See alone grants dispensation from impediments arising from sacred orders or from public perpetual VOWS of chastity in religious institutes of pontifical right (c 1078 §2). See **Forum; Occult**.

C of E. **Impediments to ordination**: the diocesan must not admit a candidate into holy orders if he or she is suffering or has been suffering from any physical or mental infirmity which will prevent him or her from 'ministering the word and sacraments or from performing the other duties of the minister's office' (canon C4(2)). The diocesan BISHOP must not admit a person who has remarried and whose former spouse is still living, or a person who is married to a divorced person whose former spouse is still living (canon C4(3)). The ARCHBISHOP of the PROVINCE on receiving an application from the diocesan bishop may grant a FACULTY for the removal of the impediment imposed by canon C4(3). **Impediments to marriage**: a person has to be sixteen

71

years of age before he or she can marry. The 'marriage' of a person under sixteen years is void (canon B31(1)). A marriage between persons who are within the degrees expressed in the Table of Kindred And Affinity included in canon B31(2) is also void. According to canon B32 no minister shall solemnize a marriage between parties 'either of whom (not being a widow or widower) is under eighteen years of age' without the Consent of a parent or guardian. A minister has a duty when an application is made to him for marriage in the Church where he is the minister, to inquire if there is any impediment to the marriage (canon B33).

IMPRIMATUR (L, let it be printed)

RC. Certification by a 'censor' who is usually appointed by the diocesan Bishop with the effect that a work on a theological or moral subject may be published. The word 'imprimatur' and the censor's name appear at the beginning or the end of the book. See **Censorship of Books.**

IMPRIMI POTEST (L, it can be printed)

RC. The approval of the authority of a religious institute, which is required before any of its theological or moral writing may be published. See **Censorship of Books**.

IMPUTABILITY (L *imputabilitas*)

RC. The attributing of moral responsibility to one who has violated the law. Imputability is grounded in malice or culpability (i.e. negligence or a lack of due diligence) on the part of the offender (c 1321). Imputability can be diminished or removed in certain circumstances (e.g. where there is ignorance or imperfect use of reason). See **Delict**.

INCARDINATION (L *incardinatio*)

RC. A juridical Act whereby a Cleric is affiliated to a Particular Church (a Diocese or equivalent), a personal Prelature, an Institute of Consecrated Life or a Society of Apostolic Life (cc 265, 266–72). A cleric is never allowed to become unattached or itinerant. See **Excardination**.

INCOLA (L)

RC. A person who lives in his or her place of Domicile (c 100).

INCUMBENT (L *incumbo*)

C of E. The holder of a Benefice upon whom certain duties are incumbent. An incumbent as a Priest having the cure of souls is required to

---

perform the following duties: to say Morning and Evening Prayer in church; to celebrate Holy Communion; to preach each Sunday; to instruct children; to prepare candidates for CONFIRMATION; to visit the sick; to consult with the PAROCHIAL CHURCH COUNCIL; and to make proper provision for his or her absence (canon C254). Furthermore, he or she is to reside in the benefice in the house provided (PA ss. 32–51; canon C25). See **Rector**; **Vicar**.

INDISSOLUBILITY (L *indissolubilitas*)

RC. A quality which (along with unity) is the very essence of all MARRIAGES, sacramental or natural (c 1056). A sacramental and consummated marriage cannot be dissolved except through death (c 1141). An unconsummated marriage between persons who have been baptized, or between a baptized person and an unbaptized person, can be dissolved by virtue of the PAULINE PRIVILEGE if, after the one person has received BAPTISM, the other person leaves the marriage (c 1143). See **Nullity**.

C of E. Marriage is a life-long union which is dissolved only by the death of one partner (canon B30(1)). In civil law a CLERIC is not under a duty to marry those legally entitled to be married in his or her CHURCH if one party is divorced with a partner still living (see MCA 1965 s. 8(2)). However, a cleric is not precluded from conducting such a marriage if his or her conscience is clear about doing so. Guidelines are issued by diocesan BISHOPS in the exercise of their *IUS LITURGICUM*.

INDUCTION (L *induco*)

C of E. The act whereby an instituted or collated PRIEST is put fully in possession of the BENEFICE and all its emoluments. It is performed by the ARCHDEACON (canon C11). See **Collation**; **Institution**.

INDULGENCE (L *indulgentia*)

RC. A remission before God of the temporal punishment for sin, the guilt of which is already forgiven (c 992). An indulgence is partial or plenary depending upon whether it frees a party either partly or totally from temporal punishment (c 993). Besides the supreme authority of the Church, indulgences can only be granted by those to whom this power has been given by the law or granted by the pope (c 995). A diocesan BISHOP can, for instance, grant a partial indulgence to persons within his DIOCESE, and a papal blessing with a plenary indulgence three times a year on solemn feasts which he designates. See Paul VI *Indulgentiarum Doctrina* (1967).

INDULT (L *indultum*)

  RC. A DISPENSATION granted by the APOSTOLIC SEE allowing a deviation from the law of the Church in a particular circumstance and for a specified period. A dispensation may be granted to a member of a religious institute; it is granted for a grave cause, usually when a crisis or a question has arisen over a particular vocation. **Indult of exclaustration**: an indult granted by a supreme moderator to a member who has made perpetual VOWS for up to three years (c 686). **Indult of departure**: a RESCRIPT granted by the competent authority, which allows a member of an INSTITUTE OF CONSECRATED LIFE who has been perpetually professed or incorporated, or a member of a SOCIETY OF APOSTOLIC LIFE who has been definitively incorporated to leave the institute or society and to cease being a member (cc 691, 727, 743). See **Rescript**.

INHIBITION (L *inhibitio*, prohibition)

  RC. A temporary prohibition from the exercise of a disputed right which is likely to infringe upon the prevailing right of another person, e.g. an INJUNCTION granted where there is a complaint of NULLITY (c 1621). An order of prohibition cannot be decreed if the harm that is feared can be repaired (cc 1496, 1498). See **Sequestration**.

  C of E. The disqualification for a specified time of a CLERIC who has committed an offence, from exercising the functions of his or her ORDER (EJM s. 49). The diocesan BISHOP may inhibit an INCUMBENT from performing his or her duties in the PARISH when there has been a serious breakdown in the pastoral relationship between incumbent and parishioners (I(VB)M s. 9A(1), (2)). The bishop may also inhibit a cleric from taking services within the DIOCESE if he or she is accused of a criminal or an ecclesiastical offence (EJM s. 77). See **Censure**.

INJUNCTION (L *injunctio*)

  RC. A positive command or a prohibitive order issued by a competent executive authority to ensure the observance of the law. It is issued for example when a group of religious disobey the repeated directives of the APOSTOLIC SEE (c 49). In complaint of NULLITY cases it is issued against the implementation of a SENTENCE on the grounds that the sentence was null (cc 1496 §2; 1620, 1621).

  C of E. An order issued by the CONSISTORY COURT either to prevent a threatened illegal act (e.g. work which is about to be carried out in a CHURCH in the absence of a FACULTY) or to restore the *status quo* following an illegal act (CCEJM s. 13(4), (5)). Failure to comply with any requirement of an injunction issued by the CHANCELLOR (unless there are reasonable grounds) is a contempt of court (FJR r. 7.2(a) and appendix). A restoration order cannot be granted in respect of a wrong which occurred more than six years prior to the application (unless the wrong has been unreasonably concealed) (CCEJM s. 13(8), (9), (10)). The power to issue an injunction concerning a CATHEDRAL lies with the VICAR general's court in each of the PROVINCES (CC(SP)M s. 5).

INSTANCE (L *instantia*)

RC. A certain level of adjudication in the prosecution of a lawsuit before a tribunal. The instance begins with the CITATION and ends with the peremption, or RENUNCIATION, or SENTENCE, or reconciliation (cc 1517, 1525, 1713). See also *LITIS CONTESTATIO*; *LITE PENDENTE*. Also, the degree of JURISDICTION: a court of the first instance, second instance, etc. An appeal from a first instance decision can be lodged with a domestic court of appeal (c 1438); appeal can also be made directly to the Roman ROTA (c 1444). A case may at any stage be directly brought before the APOSTOLIC SEE by any member of the faithful (c 1417).

INSTITUTES OF CONSECRATED LIFE (L *instituta vitae consecratae*)

RC. Institutes 'canonically established by the competent authority' where the faithful are able to live a life consecrated to God; the faithful profess vows of poverty, chastity and obedience (c 573 §2). Consecrated life is described in *CIC* as 'a stable form of living, in which the faithful follow Christ more closely under the action of the Holy Spirit, and are totally dedicated to God, who is supremely loved' (c 573 §1). *CIC* refers to two varieties: **religious institutes** and **secular institutes**. **Religious institutes** include: **clerical institute**: an institute which is governed by CLERICS 'by reason of the end or purpose intended by the founder, or by reason of lawful tradition' (c 588 §2). **Lay institute**: an institute which 'by its nature, character and purpose, its proper role defined by its founder or by lawful tradition' excludes the exercise of sacred ORDERS (c 588 §3); for example, an institute founded for the purpose of nursing. **Pontifical institute**: an institute established by, or formally approved by, the APOSTOLIC SEE (c 589). **Diocesan institute**: an institute established by the diocesan BISHOP which has not been formally approved by the Apostolic See (c 589). **Exempt institute**: an institute subject to the governance of the pope alone which is established 'with a view to the common good' (e.g. to reform the life of clerics: c 591). **Secular institutes** are institutes where the faithful live in the world and at the same time 'strive for the perfection of charity and endeavour to contribute to the sanctification of the world' (c 710). See **Exemption**; **Religious Order**; **Societies of Apostolic Life**.

INSTITUTION (L *institutio*, appointment)

RC. The placing of a PRIEST in possession of a PARISH. A priest is usually assigned to a parish by the BISHOP who freely confers on him the office of pastor (cc 523, 524). A priest is installed (instituted) as pastor by the bishop or by a priest delegated by him, e.g. the VICAR forane. The bishop can grant a DISPENSATION instead of employing the process of installation (c 527 §2).

C of E. The act whereby a priest is admitted to the cure of souls of a parish as the INCUMBENT. It is performed by the bishop (canon C10).

INSTRUCTION (L *instructio*)

RC. A document which clarifies a law and which determines how a law ought to be implemented; it may be published by one possessing executive power to a lesser administrative authority, e.g. the instructions issued by the APOSTOLIC SEE (c 34 §1). The regulations which an instruction contains must not derogate from the law (c 34 §2). An instruction ceases to have force when it is revoked by the authority which published it or by cessation of the law upon which it is based (c 34 §3). The General Instruction on the Roman Missal, unlike an instruction, is a legislative document. See **Decree**.

INTERCOMMUNION (L *intercommunio*)

RC. Catholic ministers may lawfully administer the SACRAMENTS only to Catholics, who equally may lawfully receive them only from Catholic ministers, except under certain conditions (c 844 §1). A Catholic minister may administer the EUCHARIST to other Christians not in full communion with the Catholic Church if: (i) there is either 'a danger of death' or another 'grave and pressing need'; (ii) it is impossible, physically or morally, for the persons concerned to approach a minister of their own community; (iii) the persons make a 'spontaneous' request, 'demonstrate' the Catholic faith regarding the sacrament, and are 'properly disposed' (c 844 §4). Catholics for their part may receive the Eucharist from a non-Catholic minister so long as there is real necessity or genuine spiritual advantage, and it is impossible for them to approach a Catholic minister, the Church of the non-Catholic minister has valid sacraments, and there is no danger of error (c 844 §2). For example, the sacraments of the Eastern Orthodox Churches not in communion with the APOSTOLIC SEE are recognized as valid.

C of E. Baptized persons who are communicating members of other Churches which subscribe to the DOCTRINE of the Holy Trinity are allowed to receive Holy Communion; so also are baptized persons in immediate danger of death (canon B15A). See *Communicatio in Sacris*; **Ecumenism**; **Eucharist**.

INTERDICT (L *interdictum*)

RC. One of three medicinal PENALTIES (or CENSURES), along with EXCOMMUNICATION and SUSPENSION, in *CIC*. *CIC* refers only to personal interdicts, the effects of which are largely the same as of excommunication. However, while an excommunication deprives a member of communion with the Church, an interdict forbids only certain liturgical activities (c 1332). A person who stirs up opposition to Church authority is to be punished by an interdict or other just penalty (c 1373). An interdict is also incurred when a person who is not a PRIEST attempts to simulate the Eucharistic Sacrifice or attempts to simulate hearing CONFESSION (and/or imparting sacramental ABSOLUTION: c 1378). The pope or a BISHOP can impose an interdict, depending upon the circumstances. See **Censure**; **Excommunication**; **Suspension**.

IRREGULARITY (L *irregibilis*)

RC. A perpetual IMPEDIMENT as regards the reception or exercise of ORDERS (cc 1041, 1044), e.g. commission of APOSTASY, HERESY or SCHISM.

IUS ANTIQUUM (L, old law)

RC. Church law which was to be found in the various collections of private individuals from earliest times: until the *Decretum Gratiani* (*c.* 1140) the law of the Church had to be deduced from these collections. See *Dionysiana*; *Ius Novum*.

IUS COMMUNE (L, universal law)

RC. The general and UNIVERSAL LAW of the Church of Rome common to western Christendom before the Reformation. It is not to be confused with the English system of COMMON LAW which is based upon the common CUSTOM of the land. See **Codex**; *Corpus*.

IUS LITURGICUM (L, liturgical jurisdiction)

C of E. The right to decide upon the manner and form of public worship inherent in the office of BISHOP. It enables the bishop to authorize for use in his DIOCESE what would otherwise be unlawful – for example, the widespread use of the 1928 Prayer Book in many CHURCHES at that time despite its rejection by Parliament. It forms part of the larger law which allows CUSTOM to mitigate the rigour of the law. The *ius liturgicum* survives nowdays only in the discretion which the bishop is allowed in order to resolve doubt arising from BCP. Canon B1 sets out the forms of service which are authorized for use in the Church. Clergy are bound to use only these authorized forms of service, except for the exercise of discretion regarding variations 'which are not of substantial importance in any form of service authorized by Canon B1' (canon B5: see also canons B2–4; C of E (W and D) M s. 1(5)(a)). The authority of the above canons and the judgement in the case *Re St Thomas, Pennywell* [1995] 2 WLR 154 leads Bursell to argue that 'even in the most unlikely event of a broad 'ius liturgicum' surviving until this century, it has clearly now been abrogated' (*Liturgy, Order and the Law* (Oxford, 1996), 279).

Ius Novum (L, new law)

RC. Church law which is found in codes compiled or sanctioned by the papacy. It is contrasted with the *Ius Antiquum* which was deduced from the collections of individuals. In England from the *Decretum Gratiani* (*c.* 1140) until the time of the Reformation the law of the Church was deduced from these codes. See **Decretal; Decretalist; Decretist.**

J

Juridical Person (L *persona iuridica*)

RC. A member of the faithful who collaborates in various ways in furthering the mission of the Church, e.g. by setting up associations. Since the Church is 'a moral person by divine disposition' (c 113 §1) it includes juridical persons that are 'subjects of obligations and rights which accord with their nature' (c 113 §2). According to *CIC* 'Aggregates of persons or of things which are directed to a purpose befitting the Church's mission, which transcends the purpose of the individuals, are constituted juridical persons either by a provision of the law itself or by a special concession given in the form of a decree by the competent authority' (c 114 §1). Examples of juridical persons also include charitable foundations, and structures such as Dioceses and Parishes.

Jurisdiction (L *jurisdictio*)

RC. Governance. Only those who have been ordained 'are capable of the power of governance' (c 129 § 1). For example, a Bishop possesses legislative, executive, and judicial power to govern his Diocese (c 391). Church courts have jurisdiction over cases which are concerned with spiritual matters, and over the violation of Ecclesiastical Laws. See *Munera*.

C of E. The exercise of authority in accordance with the Canons of the Church. For example, a bishop's office is one of teacher, governor and principal minister (canon C18(1), (2), (3), (4)). There is a hierarchical system of Church courts. Broadly, Church courts deal with 'civil' work (the Faculty jurisdiction) and 'criminal' work (offences against the ecclesiastical law, unbecoming conduct, and serious neglect of duty by the clergy). See **Parallel Episcopal Jurisdiction**.

L

LACUNA LEGIS (L)

RC. A gap in the law. This is evident, for instance, when there is no provision in the legal system for redressing an injustice. When there is a *lacuna* those who exercise judicial or executive power in the Church can take appropriate action to fill the gap by DECREE, SENTENCE or decision. They cannot extend this doctrine to cover penal matters. In decision making they are to have recourse to analogous cases and NORMS, general principles of law, the doctrine of EQUITY, the jurisprudence and praxis (general policies) of the Roman *CURIA*, and the common and constant opinion of learned persons (c 19). See **Analogy; Equity.**

LAICIZATION (L *laicus*, Gk λαικός)

RC. The loss of the clerical state by means of a RESCRIPT from the APOSTOLIC SEE (c 290 3°). Rescripts are granted to DEACONS only for 'grave reasons', and to PRIESTS only for 'the gravest of reasons'. The CLERIC himself may seek a rescript, or it may be sought by the diocesan BISHOP or major religious superior (even without his consent). See **Laity.**

C of E. A cleric may voluntarily relinquish the exercise of his or her ORDERS by legal PROCESS, or may be deprived of the exercise of his or her orders by legal and canonical process. Furthermore, a cleric may be deposed from orders after deprivation (canon C1(2)).

LAITY (L *laicus*, Gk λαικός)

RC. Since Vatican II the distinction between the ordained and the laity is based not upon the canonical status of the clergy and the laity, but upon recognizing sacred ministers as a group within the Christian faithful. The role of clergy and laity within the life and work of the Church is one of mutual interaction (*LG* 32). The rights and obligations of the laity are included in the section of *CIC* which covers the obligations and rights common to all the Christian faithful (cc 207–23). CANONS which refer specifically to the lay Christian faithful are relatively few (cc 224–31). For the liturgical functions which lay persons can perform, see c 230.

C of E. Strictly speaking, the laity comprise all those who have been admitted to the Church through BAPTISM. Modern usage, however, draws a distinction between the ordained clergy and laity. For the ministry of lay officers in the Church see canons E1–8. See **Cleric**; **Lay Worker**; **Order**.

LAMBETH CONFERENCE

C of E. A conference of BISHOPS worldwide which meets once every ten years, formerly at Lambeth but more recently at Canterbury, to coordinate the work of the ANGLICAN COMMUNION. It provides an opportunity for the Church as a whole to meet and to exchange opinions. Its resolutions have no legal basis, but various resolutions generally accepted by the conference have strong persuasive authority in Churches which have implemented them. The Anglican Communion comprises Churches which are in communion with the Church of England and which conform with its faith and DOCTRINE.

LAMBETH DEGREE

C of E. A degree issued by the Archbishop of Canterbury through his COURT OF FACULTIES. The academic dress of the university to which the ARCHBISHOP belongs is usually worn by recipients. The judge of the provincial courts of Canterbury and York is *ex officio* Master of the Faculties. See **Archbishop**.

LAMBETH QUADRILATERAL

C of E. A statement made by the LAMBETH CONFERENCE of 1888 which laid down four fundamental conditions for Church unity. These conditions are: the acceptance of Holy Scripture as containing all things necessary for salvation, of the Apostles' Creed and the Nicene Creed, of the two dominical SACRAMENTS of BAPTISM and the Lord's Supper, and of the historic EPISCOPATE. This statement is of great importance to ecumenical relations. See **Ecumenism**.

LAST RITES (L *ritus*)

RC. The SACRAMENT of ANOINTING OF THE SICK is given those at the point of departing this life in order to fortify them in their final hours (c 1004 § 1). The EUCHARIST is also offered to those about to leave this life as *VIATICUM*, the sacrament of passing over from death to life (cc 911, 921, 922). These two sacraments, together with the sacrament of penance (c 986 §2), prepare the Christian faithful for their home in heaven. See **Confession**.

C of E. Anointing of the Sick, Holy Communion and the sacrament of reconciliation are to be administered to the sick and dying if requested by them (canons B37(2), B37(3), B29(3)).

LATAE SENTENTIAE (L, according to the ruling given)

RC. An automatic PENALTY which is incurred by the very commission of an offence (c 1314). Such a penalty (e.g. EXCOMMUNICATION) is reserved for the most serious ecclesiastical offences where it is necessary to protect the public good (c 1318). See **Censure**; *Ferendae Sententiae*; **Sentence**.

LAY WORKER

C of E. A lay person who is authorized by LICENCE or permission of the diocesan BISHOP to perform certain duties in the Church. Only a person who has been baptized and confirmed and who is a regular communicant of the Church of England may be admitted as a lay worker. The person to be admitted must also have had the proper training and must possess the other necessary qualifications (canon E7(1)). In the place where he or she is licensed to serve and under the direction of the minister, a lay worker may lead the people in public worship, exercise pastoral care, evangelize, instruct the people in the Christian faith and prepare them for the reception of the SACRAMENTS (canon E7(3)). A lay worker may also say Morning or Evening Prayer (save for the ABSOLUTION), distribute the holy sacrament of the Lord's Supper and read the Epistle and Gospel (canon E7(4)). Furthermore, a lay worker may be authorized by the bishop at the invitation of the minister to preach at divine service, to church women, to bury the dead (with the goodwill of the person responsible) and to publish BANNS of MARRIAGE at Morning or Evening Prayer (canon E7(5)). For the admission and licensing of lay workers, see canon E8. See **Extraordinary Minister**.

LECTOR (L, reader)

RC. A minister who reads the word of God (but not the Gospel) during Mass. Laymen can be installed as lectors subject to the conditions laid down in canon 230. Before a person is promoted to the DIACONATE he is required to have been a lector or an ACOLYTE for a suitable period of time (c 1035; see also Paul VI: *Ministeria Quaedam* (1972)). See **Extraordinary Minister**.

LEGATE (L *legatus*, ambassador)

RC. An envoy of the pope. Legates fall into three categories: an **apostolic legate**, who represents the ROMAN PONTIFF to a particular Church; a **nuncio**, who represents the Roman Pontiff to a particular Church and to a civil government; and an **apostolic delegate**, who represents the APOSTOLIC SEE as a delegate or an observer at international councils, conferences or meetings (c 363). A *legatus a latere* is a CARDINAL sent by the Roman Pontiff to represent him in some solemn celebration or amongst some group of persons, as his 'alter ego' (c 358). See **Cardinal**.

LETTERS DIMISSORY (L *litterae dimissoriae*)

RC. A letter by which the ORDINARY permits another BISHOP to ordain one of his subjects to the DIACONATE or the PRESBYTERATE. The letter contains a recommendation of the candidate's worthiness. The term 'ordinary' includes a superior of a religious institute as well as the diocesan bishop (who is known as 'the proper bishop' cc 1015–23). A bishop who ordains a person who is not his subject without legitimate dimissorial letters is prohibited for a year from conferring the ORDER. The person ordained in such circumstances is automatically suspended from the order received (c 1383). See **Incardination**; **Proper**.

C of E. The granting of permission for the ORDINATION of a person to the diaconate and PRIESTHOOD outside the DIOCESE of his or her origin. He or she must bring letters dimissory from the bishop of the diocese of origin.

LETTERS OF ORDERS

C of E. Letters issued after ORDINATION to an ordained person bearing the seal and signature of the officiating BISHOP. They are required as evidence of ordination before a bishop can admit or institute a PRIEST to a BENEFICE (canon C10: 'Orders or other sufficient evidence' is required). This requirement does not apply when the priest has been ordained by the instituting bishop. See **Letters Testimonial**.

LETTERS TESTIMONIAL (L *litterae testimoniales*)

C of E. Letters which bear testimony to the good life and behaviour of a person who is to be ordained DEACON or PRIEST and which must be exhibited to the BISHOP of the DIOCESE (canon C6). A person to be made deacon must also produce a certificate 'or other sufficient evidence' of his or her place and date of birth (canon C6(1)(a)). A person to be ordained priest must also exhibit his or her LETTERS OF ORDERS to clarify his or her present clerical status (canon C6(2)(a)).

LEX NON SCRIPTA (L)

RC. The unwritten law of the Church and state which was applied by the ecclesiastical courts in pre-Reformation times. This law was derived from immemorial usage and based upon the law of Rome.

LIBELLUS (L, a petition for a juridical case)

RC. A petition presented to a competent judge by a person who wishes to bring another to court, or by the PROMOTER OF JUSTICE (cc 1501–6, 1709, 1721). The petition must explain the object of the controversy and request the judge's services (c 1502). The judge has a period of one month in which to accept or reject the petition. If the judge is silent for a further ten days the petition is considered as having been accepted (c 1506). It is exceptional for a peremptory legal deadline to refer to a court. See *Fatalia Legis*; **Instance**; *Litis Contestatio*.

LIBER CANONUM (L, book of canons)

RC. A private collection of CANON LAW by Theodore of Tarsus which formed the basis for ten canons adopted at the Council of Hertford (673) for implementation in England. The ten canons were based on canons contained in the *DIONYSIANA*.

LICENCE (L *licentia*)

C of E. A **bishop's licence** authorizes alteration or repair to a CHURCH in the DIOCESE (canon C18(4)). An ARCHDEACON can grant a licence for the temporary reordering of the interior of a church (FJR r. 8). A 'common' licence authorizes the solemnization of MARRIAGE without BANNS. A **special licence** is granted by the Archbishop of Canterbury to allow parties to a marriage to marry anywhere in England (canon B34). An **episcopal licence**, under the bishop's hand and seal, gives permission to minister in his diocese. Unbeneficed clergy and LAY WORKERS must be admitted to serve within the diocese by episcopal licence or by written permission to officiate (canons C8(3), E7(1)). See **Archbishop**; **Bishop**; **Extraordinary Minister**; **Lay Worker**; **Vicar**.

LIGAMEN (L, bond)

RC. A MARRIAGE bond. A bond which comes into existence when the parties give their CONSENT to marriage. While the bond exists the parties are juridically obliged to be faithful to each other (c 1085). The bond ceases with the death of a spouse, or when it is dissolved. A marriage which is invalid due to a diriment IMPEDIMENT can only be convalidated after the impediment has ceased or been dispensed with and the party who is aware of its existence has renewed his or her consent (c 1156). See **Dispensation**.

LITE PENDENTE (L)

RC. While a suit is pending. An act of PROCESS, when a contentious trial has been officially opened, which continues from the time a CITATION has been communicated to the parties until SENTENCE is passed. While litigation is pending, the object under dispute cannot be transferred between the parties nor altered to its detriment: *lite pendente nihil innovetur* (while a suit is pending nothing new is to be introduced: c 1512). See **Process**.

LITIS CONTESTATIO (L, entering of a suit)

RC. The defining of the terms of a controversy (or the joinder of issues). These are specified in the DECREE of the judge and are based on the petitions and responses of the parties, written or oral. Once the judge has determined the terms of a controversy the terms can only be changed through a new decree at the request of one party and for a serious reason (cc 1513–16).

LITURGY (L *liturgia*, Gk λειτουργία, service)

RC. An arrangement of rites which make up divine worship. The liturgical celebrations of SACRAMENTS and other services are celebrations of the whole body of the Church (c 837 §1). The sacred liturgy is the exercise of Christ's priestly office (c 834 §1). The Church has the right to regulate liturgy (c 838 §1). See **The Divine Office**.

C of E. Liturgical worship is an important symbol of the corporate witness of the Church. In addition to the liturgy contained in BCP (which has statutory authority), there are alternative forms of liturgy – for example, those contained in ASB (C of E (Wand D) M). Liturgical forms of services authorized for use in the Church are listed in canon B1. These include forms of service approved by the GENERAL SYNOD, and forms of service authorized by the ARCHBISHOPS for experimental periods. See **Daily Offices; Doctrine**.

M

M*AGISTERIUM* (L, instruction)

RC. The teaching role of the hierarchy of the Church. In certain instances the pope teaches with supreme and infallible authority on matters of faith and morals (see John Paul II: apostolic letter *Ad Tuendam Fidem* (1998)). The same is true of the C*OLLEGE* OF B*ISHOPS*. The college of bishops gathered in an E*CUMENICAL* C*OUNCIL* form the solemn *magisterium* of the Church. Members of the college scattered abroad make up the ordinary and universal *magisterium* of the Church (cc 337, 750). Canon 750 §2 of *CIC* states that 'each and every thing set forth definitively' by the Church's *magisterium* with regard to teaching on faith and morals must be 'firmly accepted and held' by Christ's faithful; this refers to 'things required for the holy keeping and faithful exposition of the deposit of faith'. See **Doctrine.**

M*AJOR* A*RCHBISHOP* (L *archiepiscopus maior*)

EC. The metropolitan of a S*EE* who generally has the same power as a patriarch and like him receives the *PALLIUM*. He presides over an entire church S*UI* I*URIS* which is not a patriarchate (*CCEO* cc 151, 152). See **Archbishop.**

M*AJOR* SUPERIOR (L *superior maior*)

RC. An office held by those who govern a religious institute, a P*ROVINCE* or its part equivalent, or an autonomous house. The office is also held by V*ICARS* of the above (c 620). A*BBOT* primates and superiors of monastic congregations are also considered major superiors although the authority of these offices is to be found in the proper law of the institute (i.e. their real J*URISDICTION* is over a particular monastery): they do not possess the authority given to major superiors by U*NIVERSAL* L*AW*.

M*ANDAMUS* (L, we command)

C of E. A writ issued by the High Court to enforce certain actions. For example, it may be issued to enforce the right to bury (*R* v. *Coleridge* (1819) 2 B&A1d 806) or to compel an ecclesiastical court to assume J*URISDICTION* in a particular case when it is right to do so (*R* v. *Archbishop of Canterbury* (1856) 6 E&B 546).

MARRIAGE (L *matrimonium*)

RC. A valid marriage is a life-long COVENANT between two persons, baptized or unbaptized. A sacramental marriage is a marriage between two baptized persons; it is a life-long covenant which is ordered towards the spouses' well-being, and the procreation and upbringing of children (c 1055 §1). Unity and indissolubility are 'essential properties' of marriage (cc 1056, 1134). A ratified and consummated marriage cannot be dissolved except through death (c 1141). A canonically invalid marriage can be declared null. A marriage which was canonically invalid *ab initio* can be validated by means of CONVALIDATION (i.e. the curing of IMPEDIMENTS, DEFECTS in CONSENT or lack of form). **Marriage by Proxy**: when one of the parties is hindered from being present for a valid marriage that person may appoint a proxy by special mandate to contract the marriage in his or her name (e.g. a marriage involving immigrants: c 1105). See **Advocate**; **Indissolubility**; **Nullity**.

C of E. A permanent and life-long union between two parties for their mutual well-being and for the procreation and nurture of children. It is sacramental in nature (canon B30(1)). The parties need not be baptized. A minister cannot refuse to marry on the grounds that one or other party is not baptized (*House of Bishops Guidelines for the Celebration of Mixed-Faith Marriages in Church* (1992) §2). A marriage is invalid if the parties lack legal capacity, e.g. lack of age, physical impotence, CONSANGUINITY or AFFINITY. A minister is under a canonical duty to enquire about impediments before solemnizing a marriage (canon B33). Under the Marriage Acts it is a criminal offence to solemnize a marriage outside prescribed hours and places, without publication of BANNS, etc. (MA 1949 ss. 75, 76; MA 1983 sched. 1). See **Banns**; **Licence**.

MASS OFFERING (OR STOLE FEE) (L *stips ad Missae celebrationem*)

RC. A voluntary offering given to a PRESBYTER by one of the Christian faithful in order to apply the Mass according to a definite intention (c 945 §1). The amount of the offering to be made for the celebration and APPLICATION of a Mass is determined by a meeting of the BISHOPS of the PROVINCE (c 952 §1). See cc 945–58. See **Eucharist**.

MEASURE

C of E. A form of legislation which is created by the GENERAL SYNOD (SGM s. 2(1), sched. 2 art. 6(a)(i)). It must be approved by the Sovereign in Parliament. A measure has the force and effect of an Act of Parliament and can amend or repeal such an act (C of E A(P)A s. 3 (6); SGM s. 2(2)).

METROPOLITAN CHURCH (L *ecclesia metropolitana*)

EC. A Church *Sui Iuris* presided over by a metropolitan BISHOP of a determined SEE, appointed by the ROMAN PONTIFF and assisted by a council of HIERARCHS (*CCEO* c 155 §1). The metropolitan is bound to petition the *PALLIUM* from the Roman Pontiff (*CCEO* c 156 §1).

MIXED MARRIAGE (L *matrimonium mixtum*)

RC. A MARRIAGE between a Catholic and a baptized non-Catholic (c 1124). The Catholic party is required to obtain the permission of the local ORDINARY before contracting such a marriage. If the marriage is celebrated without grant of permission the marriage is still valid although it is illicit owing to failure to properly observe the law; the parties do not incur canonical PENALTIES. However, the Catholic party is under a grave obligation to ensure that any children of the marriage are baptized and brought up in the Catholic Church (c 1125 1°). A marriage between a Catholic and a former Catholic ('who has notoriously rejected the Catholic faith') is considered to be a mixed marriage (c 1071 §2). See **Disparity of Cult; Nullity.**

C of E. Parties who marry according to the rites of the Church of England are not required to have been baptized. 'Mixed' marriages (i.e. between Anglicans and non-Anglicans) are regulated by diocesan NORMS which often incorporate the *House of Bishops' Guidelines.* Mixed marriages are not legally barred unless the union is prohibited by law, and the requirements of validity and form have not been satisfied. In the case of marriage by BANNS any parties, Christian or non-Christian, may marry in the PARISH CHURCH. However, in the case of marriage by common LICENCE it is the policy of the House of Bishops 'to refuse marriage by licence where neither party is baptized'; if one party only is baptized a statement is required 'that the other party does not reject the Christian faith and desires marriage in church'. In general, the issuing of a licence is a matter 'entirely at the discretion of the diocesan bishops'. The overriding factor is 'whether [the parties] are prepared to move towards a vision of marriage compatible with Christian understanding'. Liturgically, no omissions ought to be made from the marriage service; however, additions 'might be appropriately made in the form of a reference to the faith of the non-Christian partner' (see *House of Bishops' Guidelines for the Celebration of Mixed-Faith Marriages in Church* (1992) paras. 2, 4, 11–14, 19).

MORAL CERTAINTY

RC. A term which describes a form of certainty which lies between absolute certainty and probability. A judge in giving judgement must have moral certainty about the matter he has to decide upon (c 1608

§1). Such certainty has to be based not upon opinion in a case but upon the acts and proofs (c 1608 §2). If a judge is morally uncertain as to a judgement, he must find for the RESPONDENT unless a case 'enjoys the FAVOUR OF THE LAW' (c 1608 §4). Moral certainty 'is characterized . . . by the exclusion of well-founded or reasonable doubt and . . . it is essentially distinguished from . . . quasi-certainty; . . . it does admit the absolute possibility of the contrary, and in this it differs from absolute certainty.' It 'is understood to be objective, that is, based on objective motives': see Pius XII's Allocution to the ROTA in 1942 (*CLD* 3 607–8). See **Sentence**.

MOTU PROPRIO (L, on his own initiative)

RC. An official legislative text promulgated by the pope on his own initiative and not in response to a request. It is less formal than an apostolic CONSTITUTION. An example would be Paul VI: *Ecclesiae Sanctae* (1966). See **Papal Document; Promulgation**.

MUNERA (L, functions)

RC. The functions of Christ in which the Christian faithful participate. Vatican II describes the mission of Christ as priestly, prophetic and royal (the threefold *munera*). The mission of the Church is to participate in Christ's priestly (*munus sanctificandi*), prophetic (*munus docendi*) and royal office (*munus regendi*) (c 204). Sacred ministers share differently in the threefold *munera* on behalf of the Church, by which they teach, sanctify and govern (cc 207, 375).

MUTATIS MUTANDIS (L, necessary changes being made)

This expression is used, for example, when proposed legislation is amended.

MYRON (Gk μύρον)

EC. OIL used in the EASTERN CATHOLIC CHURCH for sacramental anointing and conferring hidden grace (*CCEO* cc 694; 758 §1). See also **Chrismation**.

N

NECESSITY (L *necessitas*)

RC. A canonical principle which can be appealed to when the law is relaxed. The relaxation of a law is granted to those who hold either judicial or executive power. This principle of relaxation is sometimes built into the rule itself; e.g. a PRIEST may not celebrate Mass without some member of the faithful being present, except for a just and reasonable cause (c 906); BAPTISM may not be conferred in a private house or a hospital unless the diocesan BISHOP so provides because of a grave cause (c 860 §§1, 2). Necessity may also provide a defence when a law or a PRECEPT is violated (c 1323).

C of E. This principle has very limited authority. It is adopted where circumstances dictate a departure from the law. For instance, RESERVATION OF THE EUCHARIST, although it has been held to be illegal, is permissible for the purpose of sick communion, through the exercise of the bishop's *IUS LITURGICUM* (*Re Lapford (Devon) Parish Church* [1954] 2 All ER 310; *Bishopwearmouth (Rector and Churchwardens) v. Adey* [1958] 3 All ER 441).

NIHIL OBSTAT (L, nothing hinders)

See **Censorship of Books**.

NOMOCANON (Gk νομοκάνων)

RC. A word used since the eleventh century to refer to canonical collections comprising both ecclesiastical and imperial laws, which have been the main source of Eastern CANON LAW since the Middle Ages. The earliest collection dates from about the sixth century and is ascribed to John Scholasticus. The most important collection is the *Nomocanon of Fourteen Titles* (*c.* 629) which reduced the fifty titles of John Scholasticus to fourteen titles. It also added other titles and included a selection from twelve Fathers of the Eastern Churches, conciliar CANONS and imperial CONSTITUTIONS. It was accepted in 982 as the UNIVERSAL LAW of the Eastern Church.

NON SUI COMPOS (L, not in control of himself)

RC. Incompetent. A person who is not legally in control of himself or herself nor responsible for his or her actions.

NORMS (L *norma*)

RC. Rules and principles. For instance, Book I of *CIC* is entitled 'General Norms' and contains principles which are common to all the CANONS in the code. It also contains definitions and general rules which apply to different areas of Church law (cc 1–203). These norms help to interpret the canons. See **Canon**.

C of E. Formulae, the nature of which is directory rather than mandatory – such formulae contain the words 'ought' and 'should'. For instance, the directive 'It is expedient that every person thus baptised should be confirmed by the Bishop so soon after his Baptism as conveniently may be; so that he may be admitted to the Holy Communion' (BCP).

NOTARY (L *notarius*)

RC. An official of the diocesan *CURIA* whose role is to give testimony (by witnessing and signing) to the authenticity of signatures and copies of official documents. The official notary of the diocesan *Curia* is the CHANCELLOR (cc 482–5). ACTS of a judicial hearing are null if they have not been signed by the notary (c 1437 §1).

C of E. Ecclesiastical Notaries who witness certain ecclesiastical events, e.g. the administering of OATHS and taking of *affidavits*. The office is held by registrars of Church courts and legal secretaries of BISHOPS. Ecclesiastical Notaries are registered and regulated by the Archbishop of Canterbury's COURT OF FACULTIES. The Court of Faculties also appoints Public Notaries.

NUNCIO (L *nuntius*)

RC. A LEGATE of the pope who represents him to a particular Church and to a civil government (cc 362–7). He holds the rank of ambassador and also has the title of Dean of the Diplomatic Corps. See **Immunity**.

NULLITY (L *nullitas*)

RC. **Nullity of marriage**: the declaring null of a MARRIAGE by means of a juridic ACT upon such grounds as DEFECT of form or lack of CONSENT or owing to the existence of a diriment IMPEDIMENT which is undispensed. A declaration of nullity, unlike a dissolution of marriage, brings an end to a marriage which was invalid. **Complaint of nullity against a judicial sentence (*Querela Nullitatis*)**: a means whereby a judicial sentence is impugned by a claim that it is suffering from a substantial defect, e.g. a SENTENCE passed by a judge who is absolutely incompetent or who was acting under force or grave fear is vitiated (c 1620). If a judge's sentence is vitiated by a curable nullity (e.g. because it does not contain reasons for his decision (c 1622)) it can be healed by correcting the error or omission that caused the nullity. Moreover, a curable nullity is automatically healed after three months if no complaint is lodged against it (cc 1465 §1; 1623). *C of E.* A marriage is null and void if the parties lacked legal capacity or if the formalities were not satisfied (canons B30–5; MCA s. 11; MA 1949 ss. 6–14). The C of E has no provision in its law to effect nullity of marriage. Annulments effective in civil law are operative for the purposes of the C of E (e.g. if the parties lacked capacity). However, certain Churches of the ANGLICAN COMMUNION operate a system for formal ecclesiastical recognition of the civil annulment of marriage. For example, in Southern Africa the Church will issue, where appropriate, an ecclesiastical declaration of invalidity of a former marriage, thus allowing the solemnization of a subsequent marriage. See **Divorce and Remarriage**.

O

OATH (L *ius iurandum*)

RC. A BISHOP, before taking canonical possession of his office, is required to make a PROFESSION OF FAITH and also to take an oath of loyalty to the APOSTOLIC SEE (c 380). CLERICS are bound by a special obligation to show reverence and obedience to the Supreme Pontiff and their own bishop (c 273).

C of E. **Oath of allegiance**: an ARCHBISHOP, BISHOP, PRIEST, or DEACON is required to take the following oath of allegiance: 'I . . . do swear that I will be faithful and bear true allegiance to Her Majesty Queen Elizabeth II, her heirs and successors according to law: So help me God.' This oath has to be taken by a priest or deacon at his or her ORDINATION, by an INCUMBENT when instituted to a BENEFICE, and by a cleric when licensed to a lectureship or preachership (canon C13(1)). **Oath of obedience**: a bishop is required to take an oath of due obedience to the archbishop (canon C14(1). A priest or deacon is required to take an oath of CANONICAL OBEDIENCE to the bishop of the DIOCESE (canon C14(3)). See **Canonical Obedience**; **Declaration of Assent**; **Profession of Faith**.

OBREPTION (L *obreptio*)

RC. 'The making of a false statement' in a petition (c 63 §2). Obreption makes a RESCRIPT invalid if 'not even one of the motivating reasons submitted is true' (c 63 §2). 'The motivating reasons' are the causes for granting the favour (e.g. the principal reasons for a DISPENSATION from priestly obligations). A rescript granted *MOTU PROPRIO* does not prove an EXCEPTION in cases of obreption. Obreption may be punishable with an ecclesiastical PENALTY (c 1391). See **Subreption**.

OBSEQUIUM (L, complaisance, submission)

RC. Religious respect or submission towards the *MAGISTERIUM*, the teaching authority of the Church, which is expected of the faithful (cc 747–55; *LG* 25).

C of E. There is no equivalent canonical provision. Clergy are required to assent to Church DOCTRINE as found in the Thirty-Nine Articles, BCP and the ORDINAL (canon C15). See **Canon**; **Canonical Obedience**.

OCCULT (L *occultus*)

RC. Not public. An occult IMPEDIMENT to MARRIAGE, unlike a public impediment, cannot be proved in the external FORUM (c 1074). Proof of a public impediment may take the form, for instance, of authentic public records or the evidence of experts. An example of an occult impediment would be CONSANGUINITY resulting from a union that was illicit.

OFFICIAL (L *officialis*)

RC. The *officialis* or judicial VICAR. A PRESBYTER whom the diocesan BISHOP is bound to appoint to judge cases with ORDINARY power. He and the bishop constitute one tribunal but he cannot judge cases which the bishop reserves to himself (c 1420 §2). His power is distinct from that of the vicar general unless the smallness of the DIOCESE or the small number of cases suggest otherwise (c 1420 §1). He is appointed for a definite period of time (c 1422) but, unlike the episcopal vicar, he does not cease from his office when the SEE is vacant (c 1420 §5). The *officialis* must be of unimpaired reputation and must hold a doctorate or at least a licentiate in CANON LAW and must be at least thirty years of age (c 1420 §4).

OIL (L *oleum*, Gk ἔλαιον)

RC. Holy oil used for sacramental anointing. In cases of NECESSITY the oil may be blessed by a PRESBYTER rather than a BISHOP, but only in the celebration of the SACRAMENT (c 999).

C of E. The oil may be blessed by a bishop or priest (canon B37(3)). See **Anointing of the Sick**; **Chrismation**.

EC. The oil may be blessed by a PRIEST in the celebration of the sacrament (*CCEO* c 741).

OLD CATHOLICS

Small groups of national Churches which in 1925 formally recognized Anglican ORDINATION, and since 1932 have been in full communion with the Church of England. These Churches were created from those Christians who at various times had seceded from the Roman Catholic Church. Old Catholics include: the Old Catholic Church in the Netherlands; the German, Austrian and Swiss Old Catholic Churches; and some small groups of Slav origin – the Polish National Church (the result of the efforts of Poles and Croats), and the Yugoslav Old Catholic Church. Old Catholics maintain the apostolic succession through the CONSECRATION of Cornelius Steenoven as Archbishop of Utrecht in 1724 by Dominique Marie Varlet, Bishop of Babylon, whose own consecration in the Roman Catholic Church was regular. Their doctrinal basis is the Declaration of Utrecht (1889). BISHOPS and other clergy in these Churches are allowed to marry.

ORATORY (L *oratorium*)

RC. A place designated for divine worship by permission of the ORDINARY which is for the benefit of a community or assembly of worshippers (whereas a CHURCH is for the use of all the faithful). Other members of the faithful may worship at an oratory with the consent of the superior (c 1223). See **Church**.

ORDER (L *ordo*)

RC. The SACRAMENT through which members of the Church become sacred ministers (cc 1008–54). There are three different grades to the sacrament – the EPISCOPATE, the PRESBYTERATE and the DIACONATE. Ordination imprints 'an indelible character' (c 1008). **Impediment of order**: an obstacle which prevents a person from receiving orders (c 1042). For example, a married man is impeded from receiving orders. CLERICS are obliged to observe CELIBACY (c 277 §1).

C of E. The threefold ministry of BISHOPS, PRIESTS and DEACONS. Ministers are ordained by bishops with prayer and the laying on of hands, in accordance with authorized forms of service (canons C1–4). Those made deacons, ordained priests or consecrated bishops are, according to the ORDINAL, 'lawfully made, ordained or consecrated, and ought to be accounted both by themselves and others, to be truly bishops, priests, or deacons' (canon A4). A minister who is in holy orders can never be 'divested of the character of his order' (canon C1(2)). See **Ordinal**.

ORDINAL (L *ordino*)

C of E. 'The Form and Manner of Making, Ordaining and Consecrating of Bishops, Priests and Deacons, according to the Order of the Church of England' (BCP; canon A4; see also ASB). See **Order**.

ORDINARY (L *ordinarius*)

RC. The title of ordinary is given to the ROMAN PONTIFF, diocesan BISHOPS (and other bishops), VICARS general, episcopal vicars, superiors of religious institutes, clerical SOCIETIES OF APOSTOLIC LIFE of pontifical right and clerical religious institutes of pontifical right (c 134 §1). For military ordinariate, see **Appendix II**.

C of E. The diocesan bishop is known as the ordinary because the JURISDICTION he exercises in his DIOCESE is derived from his ORDER, original and not delegated. 'Every bishop has within his diocese jurisdiction as Ordinary except in places and over persons exempt by law or custom' (canon C18(2)). The diocesan bishop may commit the exercise of his jurisdiction to a COMMISSARY (canon C18(3)). The diocesan bishop has the right as ordinary of celebrating ORDINATIONS and CONFIRMATIONS; he has control over CHURCH services; he has the right of granting FACULTIES or LICENCES regarding the repair etc. of churches; he has the right of consecrating new churches, of instituting to vacant BENEFICES, of holding VISITATIONS and of being president of the diocesan SYNOD (canon C18(4)). **Ordinary power**: the power or authority which a person exercises by virtue of his office and not as a delegate of a higher authority. See **Archdeacon**; **Commissary**; **See**.

ORDINATION: see **Impediment**; **Order**.

P

PALLIUM (L, covering, upper garment)

RC. A circular band of white woollen cloth with two hanging strips and marked with six dark purple crosses. It is worn by an ARCHBISHOP over his shoulders at Mass or other solemn liturgical celebrations as a symbol of his authority in communion with the Church of Rome. It may be worn only in churches within the ecclesiastical PROVINCE over which he presides as metropolitan. A formal request for the pallium must be made to the pope by the metropolitan personally or by proxy within three months of his CONSECRATION or his taking possession of his SEE (cc 353, 360, 437).

EC. Metropolitans of autonomous churches (whether of patriarchates or major archiepiscopates) receive the pallium. Metropolitans within a patriarchate or major archiepiscopate no longer receive the pallium. See **Archbishop**; **Major Archbishop**.

PANCHAYAT

A council of five (but usually more) persons assembled as a court or committee to decide on matters affecting a village or community.

AC. A local court of the pastorates of the Church in India. According to the Constitution of the United Church of South India, 'the Bishop of the diocese may where necessary appoint a local Court of Panchayat for the administration of discipline of members of the Church' with an appeal lying to the Court of the Diocesan Council (Const. XI 3–5). See also the Constitution of the United Church of North India II, V, II. 1: the Pastorate Committee is the 'primary court of discipline' for 'Church members'.

PAPAL DOCUMENT (L *documentum*)

RC. A document written by the pope which gives authoritative guidance for the understanding of what has been divinely revealed. The following are types of authoritative documents, listed in decreasing order of authority. **Apostolic constitution**: a solemn legislative text issued by the supreme authority of the Church, e.g. Vatican II: dogmatic constitution *Lumen Gentium* (1964). **Encyclical letter**: a letter written by the pope, usually for the BISHOPS and the faithful throughout the world, i.e. for the Universal Church. They are a means through which the pope pronounces non-definitive DOCTRINE on matters of faith and morals which the faithful are bound to obey, e.g. *Veritatis*

Splendor (1993). Encyclicals can be doctrinal, social or exhortatory in nature. **Encyclical epistle**: a letter addressed to a specific group or to bishops of a particular part of the Church, e.g. *Slavorum Apostoli* (1985). The distinction between encyclical letters and epistles is now usually ignored. **Apostolic exhortation**: a papal document which is exhortatory in nature, e.g. *Christifideles Laici* (1988) which stresses the particular role of lay people in the mission of the Church. **Apostolic letter**: a letter written by the pope which recalls particular events in the life of the Church, e.g. *Duodecimum Saeculum* (1987) which was published on the twelfth centenary of the Second Council of Nicaea and which reflects on the meaning of images and Christian art. **Letter**: a letter containing a message; for example, Pope John Paul II's letter in 1988 to Cardinal Ratzinger, Prefect of the Sacred Congregation for the Doctrine of the Faith, in which he speaks of the difficulties in implementing the reforms of Vatican II. **Message**: a message from the pope, such as Pope John Paul II's *Message to the People of Asia* (1981) in which he encourages the fostering of inter-religious dialogue. **Declaration**: a document of an ECUMENICAL COUNCIL or congregation of the Roman *CURIA* on such matters as DOCTRINE, Christian education, religious liberty, etc., e.g. Vatican II declaration *Dignitatis Humanae* (1965) on religious liberty. **Decree**: a legislative, administrative, or judicial PROVISION of a council or congregation which supplements or implements the law, e.g. on the life and ministry of PRIESTS (see **Decree**). **Instruction**: a document of a congregation of the Roman *Curia*, which makes clear and determines how a law ought to be implemented, e.g. instruction *Eucharistiam Mysterium* (1967) concerning the EUCHARIST. Other documents issued by the Roman *Curia* include circular letters, directories, notifications, statutes, NORMS and ordinances. For further details, see F. G. Morrisey, *Papal and Curial Pronouncements: their Canonical Significance in Light of the Code of Canon Law* (2nd edn., Ottawa, 1995). See **Instruction**; **Magisterium**; **Motu Proprio**; **Obsequium**.

PARALLEL EPISCOPAL JURISDICTION

AC. It is a principle of CANON LAW that only one BISHOP may have JURISDICTION over any one place in the ANGLICAN COMMUNION. Therefore, parallel episcopal jurisdiction, which means that two or more bishops (i.e. of the same Church or Communion) have jurisdiction in one and the same territory, is an anomaly. However, it exists – namely, in Continental Europe, where a Church of England bishop (the Bishop in Europe) and an American bishop (of the CONVOCATION OF AMERICAN CHURCHES IN EUROPE) have jurisdiction over Anglican churches, situated even in the same city (e.g. Rome, Florence, Geneva). Although the LAMBETH CONFERENCE of 1968 did deplore this state of affairs and asked for its removal, this has not been achieved. The Council of Anglican Episcopal Churches in Germany, an organization of C of E and ECUSA Churches in Germany, regards itself as a first step on the way to the removal of Anglican parallel episcopal jurisdiction on the continent.

PARISH (L. *paroecia*, Gk παροικία)

RC. A division of a DIOCESE or other PARTICULAR CHURCH (c 374 §1). It is a definite community of Christians with its own pastor who is under the authority of the diocesan BISHOP (c 515 §1). A parish may be territorial or non-territorial. **Quasi-parish**: a definite community of Christians with its own pastor which has not yet been erected as a parish (c 516 §1). See **Church**; **Vicar**.

C of E. A geographical area wherein the worshipping community is committed to the care of an INCUMBENT who has the cure of souls in conjunction with the diocesan bishop. It stands at the 'grass roots' level of the Church's hierarchical structure – below deanery, archdeaconry, diocese and PROVINCE. See **Church**; **Parochial Church Council**.

PARISH FINANCE COMMITTEE

RC. *CIC* states that each PARISH must have a finance committee in order to 'help the parish priest in the administration of the goods of the parish' (c 537). This provision enables parishioners to share responsibility for the financial affairs of the parish. The parish PRIEST must seek the advice of the committee when the law so requires; he is not bound to accept the committee's advice, but if it is unanimous he must have an overriding reason for not accepting it (c 127 §2 2°). See **Parish Pastoral Council**.

PARISH PASTORAL COUNCIL

RC. According to c 536 §1 'If, after consulting the council of priests, the diocesan bishop considers it opportune, a pastoral council is to be established in each parish. In this council, which is presided over by the parish priest, Christ's faithful together with those who by virtue of their office are engaged in pastoral care in the parish, give their help in fostering pastoral action'. Although the Parish Pastoral Council is only a consultative body, it gives parishioners an opportunity to share in the decision-making process of the Church on the PARISH level; the diocesan BISHOP lays down the NORMS by which the council is regulated (c 536 §2). See **Parochial Church Council**; **Pastoral Council**.

PARISH REGISTERS

RC. Registers for BAPTISMS, MARRIAGES and deaths and other records are to be kept by every PARISH according to the prescription of the BISHOPS' conference and the diocesan bishop (c 535 §1). The baptismal register should also include records of CONFIRMATIONS, canonical status of the faithful by reason of marriage, ADOPTION, reception of holy ORDERS, perpetual profession in a religious institute, or a change of rite (c 535 §2). Every parish is required to have its own seal. Various testimonies and ACTS which have a juridical significance are signed and sealed by the pastor (c 535 §3). Every parish is also required to have an archive for the safe keeping of parish books and other documents, which are inspected by the diocesan bishop during a VISITATION (c 535 §4). Parish ADMINISTRATORS of ecclesiastical goods have a duty to prepare inventories of both movable and immovable goods of significant value and of other goods; one copy of the inventory is to be kept in the parish archive, another in the archives of the diocesan *CURIA* (c 1283 2°, 3°).

C of E. The CHURCHWARDENS of the parish are required to keep a record of all alterations, additions or repairs to the CHURCH (canon F13(3), (4)). Register books of baptisms, confirmations, marriages and BURIALS are to be kept in every parish church (canon F11). A register book of services recording the officiating minister, preacher, the number of communicants and the collection, must be provided (canon F12). Furthermore, churchwardens have a duty to compile and maintain a terrier of land belonging to the church, an inventory of articles appertaining to the church and a log-book noting all alterations, additions and repairs to the church, its lands and articles appertaining to it (CCEJM s. 4; see also PRRM 1978). The INCUMBENT is responsible for the custody of all parish registers. When the BENEFICE is vacant this responsibility rests with the churchwardens (PRRM s. 1).

PARISH RESOLUTIONS

C of E. The resolutions passed by the PAROCHIAL CHURCH COUNCIL of a PARISH which is opposed to the ORDINATION and ministry of women as PRIESTS. Two resolutions are contained in the Priests (Ordination of Women) Measure (1993): **resolution A**: 'that this parochial church council would not accept a woman as the minister who presides at or celebrates the Holy Communion or pronounces the Absolution in the parish'; **resolution B**: 'that this parochial church council would not accept a woman as the incumbent or priest-in-charge of the benefice or as a team vicar for the benefice' (P(OW)M s. 3(1); sched. 1). Where resolution A or B is in force the PCC of a parish may pass a further resolution concerning the PROVINCIAL EPISCOPAL VISITOR under the Act of Synod: 'this parochial church council resolves to petition the diocesan bishop requesting that appropriate episcopal duties in the parish should be carried out in accordance with the Episcopal Ministry Act of Synod 1993'. This resolution, unlike the resolutions under the 1993 Measure, must be reviewed at least once every five years (EMAS s. 9(2)). See **Act**.

PAROCHIAL CHURCH COUNCIL

C of E. The PCC has an important role in the life of the PARISH. It is the Church body which discusses and decides upon parish affairs. Its functions include cooperating with and supporting the parish PRIEST in promoting the whole mission of the Church in the parish (PCC(P)M s. 2(2)(a)) and preparing the annual budget (PCC(P)M s. 7(i)). Provisions made by the deanery or diocesan SYNOD are raised and implemented. For its composition see CRR. Its powers and duties are to be found in statutes, MEASURES and CANONS: see, in particular, PCC(P)M, P(OW)M, canons F1–14.

PARTICULAR CHURCH (L *ecclesia particularis*)

RC. Territorial units of the Latin church *SUI IURIS*. The principal form of the particular Church is the DIOCESE followed by its equivalent in law – namely, a territorial PRELATURE, a territorial abbacy, an APOSTOLIC VICARIATE, an APOSTOLIC PREFECTURE and an APOSTOLIC ADMINISTRATION erected on a stable basis (c 368). See **Church**.

PARTICULAR LAW (L *ius particulare*)

RC. A law which is enacted for a specific territory, e.g. a DIOCESE, or for a particular group of the faithful, e.g. the members of an individual religious institute (c 13). See **Universal Law**.

PASTORAL COUNCIL (L *pastorale concilium*)

RC. CIC provides that 'In each diocese, in so far as pastoral circumstances suggest, a pastoral council is to be established. Its function, under the authority of the bishop, is to study and weigh those matters which concern the pastoral works in the diocese, and to propose practical conclusions concerning them' (c 511). The Pastoral Council is made up of 'clerics, members of institutes of consecrated life, and especially lay people' (c 512 §1). It is a consultative body which is to meet at least once a year (c 514 §§1, 2). See **Parish Pastoral Council**.

PATRIARCHAL CHURCH (L *ecclesia patriarchalis*)

EC. A Church presided over by a patriarch who enjoys power over all BISHOPS, (including metropolitans) and other Christian faithful of the Church over which he presides in accordance with the NORM of law approved by the Church's Supreme Authority (*CCEO* c 56). A patriarch of an EASTERN CATHOLIC CHURCH precedes other bishops, subject to the norms of precedence established by the ROMAN PONTIFF (*CCEO* c 58). The first place in the order of precedence among the ancient patriarchal SEES is given to Constantinople, and after that, Alexandria, then Antioch and Jerusalem (*CCEO* c 59 §2). A patriarch is canonically elected in the SYNOD of bishops of the patriarchal Church (*CCEO* c 63). He exercises ORDINARY and PROPER (and personal) power (*CCEO* c 78 §1).

PATRONAGE (L *patronatus*)

RC. There is no longer a right of patronage, only a right of PRESENTATION for ecclesiastical office. A right of presentation may belong to a group of persons or to a college (c 158 §2). It is the diocesan BISHOP who normally appoints to ecclesiastical office.

C of E. The right of a patron or patrons to appoint a person to a BENEFICE. This right may be vested in a person or a body corporate. Since the right of patronage is itself a form of property, it is transferable. For the transfer and exercise of rights of patronage see PM ss. 32(1), 32(2); P(B)M parts I and II.

PAULINE PRIVILEGE (L *privilegium Paulinum*)

RC. A means whereby a legitimate MARRIAGE between two unbaptized parties is dissolved in favour of the faith of one of the parties to the marriage when he or she is baptized and enters a subsequent marriage. The Pauline Privilege is dependent upon the departure of the un-baptized party, i.e. he or she no longer wishing to cohabit with the baptized party or no longer wishing to cohabit in peace without insult to the Creator (c 1143 §§1, 2). It is based upon the interpretation of the passage in St Paul (1 Cor. 7:12–15) in which he advises converts to depart if their unbelieving spouses refuse to live with them in peace. The privilege can be applied in the following cases: (i) a Catholic seeks to marry a convert to Catholicism, who was formerly unbaptized and married to an unbaptized person; (ii) a Catholic seeks to marry a convert to another Christian church who was formerly unbaptized and married to an unbaptized person; (iii) a convert to Catholicism who was formerly unbaptized and married to an unbaptized person seeks to marry a baptized or unbaptized person. See **Favour of the Law**; **Petrine Privilege**.

PECULIAR (L *peculium*)

C of E. A JURISDICTION which is outside the general scheme of jurisdiction within the Church. The jurisdiction of certain places of worship within a DIOCESE lies outside the jurisdiction of the local ORDINARY. Most peculiars have been created by means of express grant, others by operation of law. Peculiar jurisdictions in the Church include the universities of Oxford and Cambridge, and episcopal residences (extra-diocesan peculiars); CATHEDRAL CHURCHES (episcopal peculiars) since they are visitable by the local ordinary, and the royal household and royal residences, including their churches and chapels (royal peculiars). Royal peculiars include Westminster Abbey and St George's Chapel, Windsor. Such peculiars have the DEAN and CHAPTER as the local ordinary and are visitable only by the Crown as the head of the Church (see Act of Supremacy 1558 s. 7). A peculiar (but not a royal peculiar or a cathedral church) is subject to the jurisdiction of the CONSISTORY COURT (CCEJM s. 11(1); EJM s. 66(3)). A large number of peculiar jurisdictions were abolished under the Ecclesiastical Commissioners Acts of 1836 and 1850.

PENALTY (L *poena*)

RC. A sanction imposed or declared upon an offender by administrative DECREE or judicial procedure in order to repair a scandal, restore justice and reform the offender. Penalties are to be imposed as a last resort after every means of pastoral care on the part of the ORDINARY has failed (c 1341). A **just penalty**: an indeterminate penalty. *CIC* gives a judge wide discretion in the choice of penalty. He is, however, not to inflict a more serious penalty than is warranted by the seriousness of the particular case; he must not in such a situation impose a perpetual penalty (c 1349). **Perpetual penalty**: a penalty whose effect is perpetual. Such a penalty may only be imposed by means of a judicial PROCESS and not an administrative decree (1342 §7): an example would be dismissal from the clerical state (c 1336 §1 5°). See **Censure**.

PEREGRINUS (L)

RC. A 'traveller': a person who lives outside his or her place of DOMICILE or quasi-domicile (c 100). See **Acephalus**; **Incardination**; **Vagus**.

PERMANENT DIACONATE (L *diaconatus permanens*)

RC. An institution reintroduced into the Latin Church at Vatican II (*LG* 29). Its reintroduction, however, has not been made obligatory – the decision is left to each local BISHOPS' conference. According to *CIC* an unmarried candidate for the permanent diaconate must have completed his twenty-fifth year before he may be admitted to the diaconate; in the case of a married candidate he must have completed his thirty-fifth year and, in addition, have the written consent of his wife (c 1031 §2). A candidate under thirty-five years of age who aspires to the permanent diaconate must spend at least three years in 'a special house'; a candidate of more mature years, whether married or not, must spend three years following a programme of formation which may be determined by the bishops' conference (c 236). Permanent deacons, unlike other CLERICS, are: (i) not obliged to wear ecclesiastical dress; (ii) not forbidden to assume public office; (iii) not forbidden to undertake administration of goods belonging to lay people etc.; (iv) not forbidden to practise trade or commerce; (v) not forbidden to play an active role in political parties, etc. See **Deacon**; **Diaconate**.

PER MODUM ACTUS (L)

RC and EC. By means of an ACT. A juridic act, the juridic effects of which are limited to the particular situation (e.g. CCEO cc 477 §1; 541).

PETITIONER (L *petitor*)

RC. The person who institutes the action (the 'actor') for justice against the other party in a contentious PROCESS or MARRIAGE process. The other party is known as the RESPONDENT (*pars conventa*) (cc 1476–80). See **Process**; **Respondent**.

PETRINE PRIVILEGE (L *Privilegium Petrinum*)

RC. According to the Petrine Privilege a MARRIAGE between unbaptized persons, or between an unbaptized and a baptized person, or a polygamous marriage, may be dissolved 'in favour of the faith'. The pope grants a dissolution as the successor of St Peter. This privilege is an extension of the PAULINE PRIVILEGE. See **Favour of the Law**.

PIA CAUSA (L, good intention)

RC. A work done in order to assist the mission of the Church. Goods may be voluntarily left for a pious cause by a person on the occasion of death, or given to a pious cause during his or her lifetime (c 1299 §1).

PLENARY COUNCIL (L *plenarium concilium*)

RC. A council which is convened by the BISHOPS' conference of a PARTICULAR CHURCH with the approval of the APOSTOLIC SEE. Its work is usually to enact PARTICULAR LAWS (c 439 §1). See **Provincial Council**.

PONENS (OR RELATOR) (L, setter down *or* reporter)

RC. The reporting judge. The judge of a collegiate tribunal who is assigned to report on a case at the meeting of the judges and to put the SENTENCE in writing (c 1429).

POSTULATION (L *postulatio*)

RC. A process by which an electoral body can petition a candidate for ecclesiastical office who is barred from ELECTION to such office by an IMPEDIMENT. The process requires two-thirds of the votes of the electoral body. A precise formula of words is also required of those voting to ensure that they are aware that an impediment exists (c 181). PROVISION of office occurs by the DISPENSATION of the impediment and the admission of the postulate (cc 180–3). See **Provision.**

PRAETER LEGEM (or **PRAETER IUS**) (L, beyond the law).

RC. Apart from the law. A CUSTOM which is outside or beyond the written law, e.g. where the law is silent on a particular point.

PREACHING (L *praedicatio*)

RC. The proclamation of God's word during a liturgical ceremony or other occasion (e.g. a mission). Sacred ministers are to attach a great value to the task of preaching (c 762). Lay persons are allowed to preach in a CHURCH or an ORATORY under certain conditions (c 766). The preaching of the HOMILY or SERMON is reserved to PRESBYTERS and DEACONS. The mysteries of the faith and the NORMS of Christian living are to be expounded from the sacred text in the course of the homily (c 767 §1). A basic priority in preaching is to propose matters of faith and works for the glory of God and salvation of mankind. Preaching should also refer to human dignity, social responsibility and the right ordering of temporal goods (c 768 §§1, 2).

PREBEND (L *praebenda*)

RC. An ecclesiastical office to which is attached the income and other emoluments of an ecclesiastical living. *CIC* provides for such remuneration to be distributed to meet the needs of the DIOCESE (cc 1272, 1274).

C of E. An ecclesiastical office held by a prebendary, a non-resident honorary CANON. Formerly, it was an endowment in land or other income given to a CATHEDRAL to maintain a regular canon.

PRECEDENT

RC. In the Catholic Church there is no notion of binding precedent. An interpretation in a judicial decision or an administrative ACT does not have the force of law – it binds only the parties involved and affects only the matters in hand (c 16). ECCLESIASTICAL LAWS are to be understood in accordance with the meaning of words taken in their context. Where there is doubt about their meaning recourse is made to parallel passages in *CIC* (c 17). Custom is regarded as the best interpreter of laws (c 27). Judges may be guided by other judicial decisions (e.g. the decisions of the Roman Rota), but these are not binding.

C of E. A doctrine intended to impose an obligation on the judiciary to be bound by previous decisions. There is confusion over the binding force of precedent for two reasons: (i) too much weight has been attached to rules of courts of first Instance; (ii) there has been a failure to observe the difference between a judgement and *obiter dicta* (i.e. statements on a point of law which are not considered part of the decision). Precedent will not bind where the earlier statement is *obiter*, or where a decision is by a Provincial Court of another Province, or where a decision is by a court of co-ordinate Jurisdiction, or where an earlier decision has been disapproved of or overruled.

Precept (L *paeceptio*)

RC. An order issued to an individual or individuals requiring compliance with the law. It is an administrative Act issued by a person possessing executive power (c 35). **Singular precept**: a Decree which enjoins a determined person or persons (including Juridical Persons) to do or to omit something particularly concerning the observance of a law (c 49); e.g. an Injunction issued towards a group of parochial dissidents who are opposing and obstructing the installation of a pastor. **Penal precept**: a precept to which is attached a canonical or lighter sanction (c 1344). See **Decree**; **Obreption**; **Rescript**; **Subreption**.

Prelate (L *praelatus*)

RC. The Ordinary of a Prelature who has the right to erect a seminary and who is responsible for the spiritual formation, Incardination, Ordination, support, etc. of Clerics who make up the prelature (c 295). A **territorial prelate** is one who governs a territorial prelature en-trusted to him for a special reason (c 370). See **Diocese**.

Prelature (L *praelatura*)

RC. Personal prelature: a specialized administrative unit erected by the Apostolic See to incardinate secular Priests who then are no longer associated with any Particular Church. A personal prelature promotes an appropriate distribution of priests who can respond to particular pastoral or missionary needs (c 294). The prelature is presided over by a Prelate as its proper Ordinary (c 295 §1). Lay persons can share in the apostolic work of the prelature although they would not form the 'proper people' of the prelature (c 296). *Opus Dei* is an example of a personal prelature. **Territorial prelature**: 'a certain portion of the people of God which is established within certain territorial boundaries and whose care, due to special circumstances, is entrusted to some prelate or abbot who governs it as its proper pastor, like a diocesan bishop' (c 370). A Military Ordinarate is an example of a territorial prelature. See **Diocese**; **Excardination**; **Prelate**; **Appendix II**.

PRESBYTER (L, Gk πρεσβύτερος)

RC. A PRIEST. A CLERIC who belongs to the sacred ORDER of the PRESBYTERATE. As pastor of his PARISH he exercises pastoral care in the community. His duties are to teach, sanctify and govern (c 519). A presbyter must be a person of sound doctrine and moral integrity with a zeal for souls (c 521 §2). He must be able to administer the SACRAMENTS (cc 835 §2; 843; 530), preach the Gospel (cc 757; 762) and carry out parish administration (c 532) as required by UNIVERSAL LAW. When a team of priests are given the pastoral care of a parish only their moderator is placed in possession of the parish. The other priests are required to make a PROFESSION OF FAITH (c 542 §3). See **Presbyteral Council**; **Presbyterate**; **Vicar**.

PRESBYTERAL COUNCIL (L *presbyteralis concilium*)

RC. An assembly of PRIESTS in each DIOCESE who through consultation and advice help the BISHOP to govern his diocese (c 495). The bishop is obliged by UNIVERSAL LAW to consult the council on any significant matter (c 500 §2). The council has no authority to act without the bishop (c 500 §3). See cc 495–501. See **Presbyter**.

PRESBYTERATE (L *presbyter*, Gk πρεσβύτερος)

RC. The second grade within the SACRAMENT of ORDERS, between the DIACONATE and the episcopacy (c 1009 §1). See **Presbyter**; **Priest**.

PRESENTATION (L *praesentatio*)

RC. The right of a patron to present a candidate for an ecclesiastical office, e.g. as a BISHOP, a pastor of a PARISH (cc 147, 158–63, 377). The right of presentation is part of the right of PATRONAGE.

C of E. The right of a patron to present his nominee to the bishop when a BENEFICE becomes vacant in order for him or her to be put in possession of the cure of souls. The right of presentation is dependent upon the approval of the parish representatives and the bishop (P(B)M s. 11(1); canons C9, C10). See **Induction**; **Institution**; **Patronage**.

PRIEST (L *sacerdos*, Gk ἱερεύς)

C of E. A CLERIC who belongs to the sacred order of priests (canon C1). He or she is to preach the Word of God and to administer Holy

Communion (see **Ordinal**). A priest (as well as a Bishop and Deacon) is obliged to say the Daily Offices and to celebrate or be present at the celebration of Holy Communion on all Sundays and main Feast Days (canon C26(1)). A priest and his or her family are to be examples of godly living (canon C26(2). A priest ministering in a Diocese must first have taken an Oath of Canonical Obedience to the bishop of the diocese (canon C14, and have made a Declaration of Assent (canon C15). **Incumbent**: the holder of a Benefice: see **Rector**; **Vicar**. **Priest-in-Charge**: a priest who does not hold a Freehold office (along with an assistant Curate, Chaplain, team Vicar, etc). He or she is licensed to officiate by the bishop. See **Priesthood**.

Priesthood

C of E. One of the three Holy Orders in the Church (canon C1). See **Priest**; **Ordinal**.

Primate (L *primatus*, first rank)

RC. A title which is a prerogative of honour and which does not normally carry with it the power of governance (c 438). A **primatial see** is one which has a special historical (and certain jurisdictional) importance within a nation (e.g. the See of Armagh in Ireland). One of the pope's many titles is Primate of Italy.

C of E. The Archbishop of a Province. The Archbishop of Canterbury and the Archbishop of York are styled as 'Primate of All England and Metropolitan' and 'Primate of England and Metropolitan' respectively (canon C17(1)). They are appointed by the Crown. Of the other Churches of the Anglican Communion the law of ECUSA most comprehensively defines the role of a primate. This role includes: having responsibility in initiating, developing and implementing the policy and strategy of the Church; proclaiming the Word of God to the Church and to the world; ensuring adequate Bishops; calling together and presiding over meetings of the House of Bishops and of the General Convention; and visiting every Diocese (ECUSA Const. art. 1; Cons. I 2). The Constitutions of a number of other Churches follow the main elements of the system in ECUSA (e.g. Brazil). Primates of most of the other Churches are elected by a central Church assembly (e.g. Scotland where the Primus is elected by the Episcopal Synod). See **Bishop**; **Diocese**.

Primates' Meeting

AC. A conference of the Primates of all independent Provinces of the Anglican Communion, meeting between the Lambeth Conferences, reaffirmed by the Lambeth Conference in 1998. See **Primate**.

Prior Bond (L *vinculum prius*)

    RC. An Impediment to a Marriage due to the bond of a previous valid marriage which still exists in law (c 1085 §1). See **Pauline Privilege.**

Privation (L *privatio*)

    RC. Removal from office as a Penalty for an offence; it may be imposed by Decree or judicial Sentence (c 196).

Process (L *processus*)

    RC. Judicial procedures prescribed by law which are to be observed in settling legal disputes (e.g. the judge, the petition, the action, the formulation of doubt, the proof, the publication, the discussion, the reasoned Sentence: see Book VII of *CIC*. **Contentious process**: the ordinary and oral processes. The **ordinary process** is a trial involving Petitioner and Respondent, following a written procedure (cc 1501–1655). The **oral process** is simpler with a view towards an expeditious hearing (cc 1656–70). **Penal or criminal process**: this process is used to punish one who has committed a serious breach of Church faith or order. The Promoter of Justice acts as petitioner before the tribunal (cc 1717–31). **Documentary process**: a summary procedure whereby a judge can declare the Nullity of a Marriage with the intervention of the Defender of the Bond where there is proof of an existing Impediment or a Defect of legitimate form (cc 1686–8). **Special process**: this is employed in cases declaring nullity of marriage (cc 1671–1707) and also in cases for declaring nullity of Ordination (cc 1708–12).

Proctors of the Clergy (L *procurator*)

    C of E. Representatives of the clergy who are elected on a diocesan basis to represent them in the lower houses of the Convocations of Canterbury and York.

Procurator (L)

    RC. One who by legitimate mandate represents a party in a judicial trial (cc 1481–90).

Profanation (L *profanatio*)

    RC. The improper use of sacred things which are destined for divine worship through Dedication or a blessing (c 1171). If profanation of a sacred place occurs and is so serious in the judgement of the local Ordinary as to prevent public worship then an act of public penance is necessary to remedy the harm (c 1211). Profanation of sacred things, movable or immovable (e.g. a Church or a chalice) is punishable with a just PENALTY (c 1376). See **Blasphemy**; **Heresy**; **Sacrilege**.

C of E. CHURCHWARDENS and those who assist them, according to canon F15(1), 'shall not suffer the church or chapel to be profaned by any meeting therein for temporal objects inconsistent with the sanctity of the place'.

PROFESSION OF FAITH (L *professio fidei*)

RC. A special profession which is required from those who are about to take up particular offices or positions in the Church. CARDINALS, BISHOPS, diocesan ADMINISTRATORS, VICARS general, episcopal vicars, judicial vicars, PRIESTS, DEACONS, superiors of religious institutes, professors of theology, etc. are required to make a profession according to a formula approved by the APOSTOLIC SEE (c 833). A new formula, accompanied by an OATH of fidelity, was published on 27 February 1989.

C of E. See **Declaration of Assent**.

PRO INFECTIS (L, as if undone)

RC. An act or decision which attempts to judge the pope is considered non-existent (*pro infectis*) (c 1406 §1). 'The First See is judged by no one' (c 1404). The pope, being the supreme judge in the Church, cannot be judged by any human power. The pope alone has the right to judge heads of state, CARDINALS, LEGATES of the APOSTOLIC SEE, BISHOPS (in penal cases), and other cases which he has decided to reserve to himself (c 1405 §1). Only a judge (or any other body) who has received the prior mandate of the pope himself can review a papal decision (c 1405 §2).

PROLOCUTOR (L, advocate)

C of E. A member elected from each of the lower houses of the CONVOCATIONS OF CANTERBURY AND YORK to preside over it and to act as its representative to the corresponding upper house.

PROMOTER OF THE FAITH (L *promotor fidei*)

RC. A PRELATE theologian who is a member of the Congregation for the Causes of Saints. When a cause for CANONIZATION is in progress he is chosen from within the congregation in order to: preside over the assembly of theologians; report on the assembly itself; and to be present at the session of the CARDINALS and BISHOPS in an expert capacity only. See **Beatification**; **Canonization**; **Venerable**; **Appendix I**.

PROMOTER OF JUSTICE (L *promotor iustitiae*)

> **RC.** A diocesan OFFICIAL appointed by the BISHOP to intervene in penal cases and also in contentious cases which affect the public good (cc 1430, 1431). See **Defender of the Bond.**

PROMULGATION (L *promulgatio*, publishing)

> **RC.** The means whereby a law comes into existence in the Church and is made known to the faithful. A law comes into existence when it is promulgated (c 7). Laws of the APOSTOLIC SEE are usually promulgated through publication in the *Acta Apostolicae Sedis*, its official periodical. See **Acta.**
>
> **C of E.** The royal licence and assent is necessary before a CANON can be promulgated (SCA).

PROPER (L *proprius*)

> **RC.** An individual's pastor and diocesan BISHOP is determined by the individual's place of residence (c 107). The spiritual care of a person is allocated to his or her territorial PARISH within the diocesan territory. **Proper power:** the power or authority exercised by a person himself as opposed to vicarial power which is exercised by another on his behalf. See **Ordinary.**

PROPRIO VIGORE (L, by its own power)

> **C of E.** By the due weight of a decision. Judges are bound by an earlier judicial decision *proprio vigore*, since judicial decisions enjoy the status of law. See **Precedent.**

PROTOPRESBYTER (Gk πρῶτοπρεσβυτερος)

> **EC.** A PRESBYTER who is placed over a district consisting of several PARISHES (*CCEO* c 276 §1). His equivalent in *CIC* is the VICAR forane or ARCHPRIEST.

PROTOSYNCELLUS (Gk πρωτοσύγκελλος, sharer of the first cell)

> **EC.** A PRESBYTER (usually celibate) who is appointed by the eparchial BISHOP to assist him in governing the whole EPARCHY. He is endowed with ORDINARY vicarious power (*CCEO* cc 245; 247 §§1, 2). His equivalent in *CIC* is the VICAR general. See **Syncelli.**

PROVINCE (L *provincia*)

> **RC. Ecclesiastical province:** a grouping of a number of neighbouring DIOCESES within a defined territory in order 'to promote ... a common pastoral action of various neighbouring dioceses, and the more closely

to foster relations between diocesan Bishops' (c 431 §1). Exempt dioceses exist only by EXCEPTION and are to be discontinued (c 431 §2). Such dioceses (e.g. that of Switzerland) are immediately subject to the APOSTOLIC SEE. A metropolitan BISHOP who presides over an ecclesiastical province is ARCHBISHOP within his own diocese (c 435). **Religious province**: the primary internal division of an INSTITUTE OF CONSECRATED LIFE; 'it is the union of several houses which constitutes an immediate part of the same institute under the same superior and has been canonically established by lawful authority' (c 621). The authority of the superior is not to prejudice the authority of the Supreme Moderator of the institute.

C of E. An archiepiscopal area of oversight by a PRIMATE or metropolitan. The grouping of a number of dioceses within a defined geographical area under the governance of an archbishop (i.e. Canterbury or York). This has been defined for Churches of the ANGLICAN COMMUNION as 'a self-governing Church composed of several dioceses operating under a common Constitution and having one supreme legislative body' (ACC 4, 1979). The preamble to the CONSTITUTION in Uganda states that 'Dioceses should be associated in Provinces presided over by an Archbishop . . . for furtherance of fellowship, comity and mutual support among them'. The constitution in Sudan goes on to state that the PROVINCE is 'a combination under the Archbishop and a General Synod of the Several Dioceses in the Republic of the Sudan' (Const. art. 1). See **Bishop**; **Exemption**.

PROVINCIAL COUNCIL (L *concilium provinciale*)

RC. A council which is convened for all the PARTICULAR CHURCHES of a PROVINCE in order to enact PARTICULAR LAWS. The approval of the APOSTOLIC SEE is not required unless the territorial limits of the ecclesiastical province and the country coincide (cc 439 §2; 440). See **Plenary Council**.

PROVINCIAL COURTS

C of E. **The Court of Arches** and **Chancery Court of York**: these courts hear appeals from the CONSISTORY COURTS, in the PROVINCES of Canterbury and York respectively (EJM s. 7 (1)). See **Dean of the Arches**. **Court of Faculties**: the court of the Archbishop of Canterbury which has power to grant DISPENSATIONS. The work of the court includes granting special MARRIAGE licences and issuing LAMBETH DEGREES. See **Court of Faculties; Faculties**.

PROVINCIAL EPISCOPAL VISITOR

C of E. A BISHOP appointed by an ARCHBISHOP as his suffragan in order to carry out episcopal duties in PARISHES within the PROVINCE which are opposed to the ORDINATION and ministry of women as PRIESTS. There are two provincial episcopal visitors in the province of Canterbury – the Bishops of Ebbsfleet and of Richborough, while there is one in the province of York – the Bishop of Beverley. Arrangements for alternative episcopal oversight are set out in the Episcopal Ministry Act of Synod (1993). This Act applies when a PARISH RESOLUTION has been passed under the P(OW)M. See **Act; Parish Resolutions.**

PROVISION (L *provisio officii*)

RC. The granting of ecclesiastical office (e.g. the ELECTION of a BISHOP) by a competent ecclesiastical authority according to the NORMS of CANON LAW. An ecclesiastical office can only be validly acquired by canonical provision (c 146). Canonical provision occurs by free conferral, or by installation (if preceded by PRESENTATION), or by CONFIRMATION (if preceded by ELECTION or POSTULATION), or by election or postulation (if confirmation of office is not required) (c 147; also cc 146–83).

PROVOST

C of E. The INCUMBENT where a PARISH CHURCH has been designated a CATHEDRAL at the creation of a new DIOCESE. Such a cathedral has its own CONSTITUTION and statutes which provide for the maintenance of its dual role as cathedral and a parish church. It also has its own CHAPTER of which the BISHOP may be a member (CM s. 8(a)). The provost is appointed by the bishop who is usually the patron of the BENEFICE. See **Dean; Patronage.**

PULPIT (L *pulpitum*)

RC. A place in a CHURCH where the HOMILY is preached. The fixed ambo in the sanctuary may also be used for the homily as well as for prayers and readings from Holy Scripture – see SCDW instruction on the Roman Missal (1970) §272.

C of E. A place in a church for preaching the SERMON (canon F6). The PAROCHIAL CHURCH COUNCIL is responsible for providing and maintaining the pulpit (canon F14).

Q

QUEEN ANNE'S BOUNTY

C of E. A corporation established under the Queen Anne's Bounty Act, 1703 in order to receive from Queen Anne all her revenue of FIRST FRUITS AND TENTHS with the purpose of providing financial assistance for the clergy officiating in the Church. Whenever a BENEFICE was sequestered for non-residence such portion of its profits as the BISHOP ordered was paid for the purposes of the Bounty (PA s. 54). The Bounty also received money from the sale of parsonage houses and GLEBE. In 1947 the functions, rights and privileges of the Bounty became vested in the Church Commissioners and all property held on trust for the Bounty after that date was held in trust for the Commission (Church Commissioners Measure, 1947 ss. 1, 2).

QUERELA NULLITATIS (L)

RC. Plaint of NULLITY. A challenging of the nullity of a procedural ACT. Such an act is made valid by the judgement itself so long as three conditions are satisfied: the case must concern 'the good of private individuals'; the nullity must be one 'by positive law', e.g. when a NOTARY has failed to be present at a hearing and to sign the acts (c 1437 §1); and the party making the plaint must have known about the nullity and the nullity 'was not raised with the judge before the judgement' (c 1619). A plaint of nullity is to be distinguished from an appeal against a judgement (cc 1619–27. See **Sentence.**

QUOD NON EST IN ACTIS NON EST IN MUNDO (L, what is not in the acts is not in the world)

RC. What is not found in the ACTS has no real existence. All the information which a judge receives from the parties, or the ADVOCATE or others, must be included in the acts of the case. Opinions or private information received by a judge cannot be considered in deciding upon a case unless they are formally incorporated into the case (cc 1604 §1; 1608 §2). See **Moral Certainty.**

QUOTA

C of E. A form of taxation levied by a DIOCESE upon its PARISHES in order to meet diocesan expenditure. Parishes are asked to pay their quota, according to their ability, towards the Maintenance of Ministry Fund and other funds of the diocese. Parishes are informed well in advance what their quota payment will be for the coming year in order to enable PAROCHIAL CHURCH COUNCILS to produce their budgets. Similarly, dioceses are asked to contribute to the Church's Central Board of Finance in order to cover the expenditure of the GENERAL SYNOD. In the Church of England the quota is a voluntary tax. However, in other Churches of the ANGLICAN COMMUNION there is a canonical obligation to pay it (e.g. in the Protestant Episcopal Church in the United States of America, and in New Zealand).

R

RATIO DECIDENDI (L, reason for a decision)

C of E. The reasoning behind a decision – the decision and resultant rule of law. The only part of a previous case which is binding. According to the doctrine of PRECEDENT a court is bound to follow a case which a higher court has decided and appellate courts are bound by their previous decisions. See *Stare Decisis*.

READER

C of E. A lay person who is licensed to conduct religious services. His or her duties include: the reading of Morning and Evening Prayer (except the ABSOLUTION), and the Litany; the publishing of BANNS of MARRIAGE; the distributing of the consecrated bread and wine at the EUCHARIST; officiating at the BURIAL of the dead; and PREACHING. The diocesan BISHOP formally admits a person to the office of reader. See canons E4–6; B11–12. The office of reader in the C of E combines the offices of lay reader, lay Eucharistic minister, lay preacher and pastoral leader in the ECUSA.

RECEPTION INTO THE CHURCH

RC. A baptized member of another Church (i.e. a non-Catholic ecclesial community) seeking admission to the Church is required to make a PROFESSION OF FAITH and also to receive the rite of CONFIRMATION, even if he or she has been confirmed previously. Such a member is not to be baptized conditionally unless the validity of his or her BAPTISM is in doubt (c 869 §2). A 'convert' (i.e. a previously unbaptized person) would, of course, also need to be baptized. The service of reception is preceded by a period of instruction in the faith (usually twenty weeks) and is dependent upon the BISHOP's permission. The service is conducted by a PRESBYTER or the bishop. See Paul VI: *Unitatis redintegratio* (1964).

C of E. A person desiring to be received into the Church who has been baptized but not confirmed by a bishop is required, after instruction, to be confirmed (canon B28(2)). Any such person who has been confirmed by a bishop shall, after instruction and with the bishop's permission, be received into the Church. The bishop of the DIOCESE or his COMMISSARY is to receive a person who is a PRIEST (canon B28(3). See **Baptism**; **Confirmation**.

RECTOR (L, governor)

RC. **Rector of a church**: a PRESBYTER who is given the care of a CHURCH which is non-parochial, non-capitular (i.e. a church belonging to a CHAPTER of CANONS) and which is not associated with a religious community or a SOCIETY OF APOSTOLIC LIFE. The office in itself just involves the care of a church building with no parochial responsibility or cure of souls (cc 516, 556–63). **Rector of a seminary (or university)**: his responsibilities include the daily administration of the seminary and the performance of the students and teachers (cc 239, 260–1.

C of E. A style given to a PRIEST who has been appointed to a BENEFICE. Historically, the style 'rector' was given to a clergyman who was supported by income from the tithe and GLEBE land of a PARISH which had always belonged to the benefice. Where such emoluments had belonged (for example) to a religious house, a VICAR or deputy had to be appointed to carry out the cure of souls. See **Benefice**; **Incumbent**; **Vicar**.

RED-LETTER DAYS

C of E. Greater festivals in the Church's year which used to be printed in church calendars in red ink. Collects and readings are provided for these FEAST DAYS. See **Black-Letter Days**; **Rubrics**.

RELIGIOUS ORDER (L *ordo religiosus*)

RC. An institute or congregation of religious life. For example: **monastic orders**: Benedictines, Cistercians, etc., **mendicant orders**: Dominicans, Franciscans, etc. See **Institutes of Consecrated Life**.

C of E. Religious communities, such as Anglican Franciscans and Anglican Benedictines, who live under a rule of life. See *A Directory of the Religious Life* (4th edn., London, 1990).

REMOVAL FROM OFFICE

RC. The manner of procedure in removing pastors is set out in detail in canons 1740–7. The Second Vatican Council rendered all pastors movable (*Christus Dominus*, 31). The diocesan BISHOP may determine the length and renewability of a pastor's term of office with the approval of the bishops' conference. Such term of office is usually for six years.

C of E. CLERICS can be removed from office for offences committed against the ECCLESIASTICAL LAWS (i.e. for offences concerning DOCTRINE, ritual and ceremonial; also for offences concerning their conduct or their neglect of duty) under EJM 1963 s. 14(1)(a), (b). Clerics can also be removed when there has been a serious breakdown of the pastoral relationship in BENEFICES (I(VB)M 1977 ss. 4, 11(2)(a), 12(2)).

RENUNCIATION (L *renuntiatio*)

RC. A voluntary resignation from an ecclesiastical office 'for a just reason' (c 187). A resignation is only valid if it is put in writing or made orally in the presence of two witnesses (c 189 §1). A voluntary resignation is to be distinguished from AMOTION or removal from ecclesiastical office.

RES INTEGRA (L)

RC. A matter which is still whole, i.e. which is not yet before the court.

RES IUDICATA (L, matter decided)

RC. A case which has been irrevocably adjudged and which cannot be opened again by any court in ordinary procedure (c 1641). It results, for example, where an appeal has not been lodged within the time limit. The only recourse available is reinstatement: see *Restitutio in Integrum*.

RESCRIPT (L *rescriptum*)

RC. A reply to a request (c 59 §1). A written response by a competent administrative authority by which a privilege, DISPENSATION or other favour is granted (cc 59–75); for example, a PRESBYTER might enjoy the privilege of a private chapel. See **Decree; Obreption; Precept; Subreption**.

RESERVATION OF THE EUCHARIST (L *Eucharistiae asservatio*)

RC. The blessed SACRAMENT must be reserved in the CATHEDRAL CHURCH and in every PARISH church (c 934). The purposes of reservation are: communion for the sick and the dying, devotion to Christ who is present in the blessed Sacrament, and the distribution of Holy Communion if the need arises. The blessed Sacrament is usually reserved in a TABERNACLE.

C of E. Articles 25 and 28 of the Thirty-Nine Articles of Religion (BCP) forbid reservation of the Sacrament, and a RUBRIC in the BCP Communion service requires that any of the consecrated elements left over at the end of the service be consumed. This rubric however, only applies to a celebration according to the 1662 rite. The ASB rubrics (49 of Rite A and 42 of Rite B) do not require consumption of the remaining elements. Nowadays, the Sacrament is reserved in all cathedrals and in many churches – usually for distribution to the housebound, the sick and the dying – and this is lawful provided it has been episcopally approved. The consecrated elements are usually reserved in an AUMBRY. See **Adoration of the Eucharist; Eucharist;** *Ius Liturgicum*.

RESPONDENT

RC. The party who is cited in an action brought by the PETITIONER (the 'actor') in a contentious trial (cc 1476–80). See **Process**.

RESTITUTIO IN INTEGRUM (L, restoration to its former condition)

RC. Reinstatement. A legal remedy for a person who has been seriously injured by a clearly unjust judicial SENTENCE; such a person can be restored for reasons of natural EQUITY to his or her former situation by a competent judge. The remedy is granted against a sentence which has become a *RES IUDICATA* provided the injustice can be clearly proved (c 1645).

ROGATION DAYS (L *rogatus*, request)

RC. Rogation Days were replaced in 1969 with periods of prayer (and in 1970 with suitable Masses) for the same intentions at different times of the year to be determined by conferences of local BISHOPS. See **Ember Days**; **Fasting and Abstinence**.

C of E. The Monday, Tuesday and Wednesday following the fifth Sunday after Easter (i.e. before Ascension Day). According to the BCP they are to be kept as days of FASTING or ABSTINENCE. On these days prayers are offered for God's blessing on the fruits of the earth and the labour of human hands.

ROMAN PONTIFF (L *Pontifex Romanus*)

RC. The pope. He is the successor of St Peter, with the same role and authority. He is also referred to as the head of the COLLEGE OF BISHOPS, Vicar of Christ and Pastor of the Whole Church (c 331); these titles correspond with his mission within the universal Church. Additional titles which specify his role on a local level are Patriarch of the West, Primate of Italy, and Archbishop and Metropolitan of the Province of Rome. The Roman Pontiff has 'supreme, full, immediate and universal ordinary power in the Church, and he can always freely exercise his power' (c 331). The Roman Pontiff may resign from office, though no pope has done so since Celestine V in 1294; it is not necessary that the Pope's resignation be accepted by anyone (c 332 §2). The Roman Pontiff's power by virtue of his office is over all particular Churches and their groupings (e.g. DIOCESES, PROVINCES) as well as over the universal Church (c 333 §1). He is given this power in order to aid and support local BISHOPS. The Roman Pontiff in exercising his office as Supreme Pastor is 'always joined in full communion with the other Bishops and indeed with the Universal Church'. He may exercise this office personally or collegially (c 333 §2). See ***Magisterium***. For the ELECTION of a Roman

Pontiff, see John Paul II: apostolic constitution *Universi Dominici Gregis* (1994).

ROTA (L, wheel)

RC. An ecclesiastical tribunal. **Roman Rota**: a Roman DICASTERY and the main appellate court of the Roman CURIA. It is so called because of its system for determining its composition of judges (in panels of three, five or seven, or as a panel of the whole body). It hears second-or-third-INSTANCE cases which are non-administrative (cc 1443, 1444). It has a right in first instance to judge contentious cases regarding BISHOPS, ABBOT primates or abbot superiors of monastic congregations, and supreme moderators of religious institutes of pontifical right. It can also judge cases which concern DIOCESES or other ecclesiastical persons, physical or juridic, who are without a superior below the ROMAN PONTIFF (c 1405 §3).

RUBRICS (L *rubrica*)

C of E. The directions, instructions, rules, etc. of a service book such as BCP and ASB. They are so called because of the red ink in which rubrics were formerly printed. **Mandatory rubrics**: rubrics which govern a certain practice in the Church, e.g. 'every Parishioner shall communicate at least three times in the year, of which Easter to be one' (BCP). **Directory rubrics**: rubrics which are directives for the clergy; they are to be 'interpreted liberally according to the occasion' (*Bishopwearmouth (Rector and Churchwardens)* v. *Adey* [1958] 3 All ER 441 at 444 per G. Moore Ch). An example is the rubric at the end of the service of Holy Communion in BCP, which is meant to avoid PROFANATION of the SACRAMENT. Rubrics have the sanction of Parliament, and prevail over CANONS in cases of conflict (*R* v. *Dibdin* [1910] P 57 at 138 per Farwell J). In some Churches of the ANGLICAN COMMUNION (e.g. in Brazil) rubrics are classified as 'law'.

RURAL DEAN (or **AREA DEAN**)

C of E. A PRIEST appointed by the diocesan BISHOP to supervise a deanery (a collection of neighbouring PARISHES) for the purpose of reporting matters of concern to the BISHOP or ARCHDEACON. Such matters include cases of serious illness or distress among the clergy, and the vacancy of BENEFICES (canon C23(1)); failure to prepare and maintain a church ELECTORAL ROLL, failure to form a PAROCHIAL CHURCH COUNCIL or to hold an annual PCC Meeting (canon C23(2)). The rural dean is obliged to inform the ARCHDEACON of serious defects in the fabric, ornaments and furniture of a CHURCH in the deanery (canon C23(3)). During a vacancy in the deanery he and the CHURCHWARDENS, are sequestrators of the benefice (C of E (MP)M s. 1(1)). In the absence of the archdeacon the rural dean may give INDUCTION; he does so on the mandate of the archdeacon. He is joint chairman of the deanery SYNOD (canon C23(4)). See **Sequestration**; **Vicar**.

S

SACRAMENTAL FORM (L *forma sacramentalis*)

   RC. The essential words or formula necessary for the validity of a SACRAMENT. It belongs to the Church's Supreme Authority (i.e. the pope or an ECUMENICAL COUNCIL) to decide on what is required for the valid celebration of a sacrament (c 841).

SACRAMENTALS (L *sacramentalia*)

   RC. Sacred signs, somewhat in imitation of the SACRAMENTS, by which spiritual effects are signified and obtained through the intercession of the Church (c 1166). Examples include CONSECRATIONS, DEDICATIONS, EXORCISMS, blessings, alimony and the Liturgy of the Hours (cc 1169–72).

SACRAMENTS (L *sacramenta*)

   RC. These 'actions of Christ and of the Church' are 'signs and means by which faith is expressed and strengthened, worship is offered to God and . . . sanctification is brought about' (c 840). The seven sacraments are: BAPTISM, CONFIRMATION, EUCHARIST, CONFESSION, ANOINTING OF THE SICK, ORDER and MARRIAGE. Matters dealing with the lawful celebration, administration, reception, etc. of the sacraments are decided upon either by the Church's supreme authority or by the conferences of BISHOPS or by the diocesan bishops.

   C of E. There are two sacraments 'generally necessary to salvation': BAPTISM and the Lord's Supper (BCP Catechism). A CANON which deals with the administration of the sacraments may not be presented for final approval to the GENERAL SYNOD unless it has first been approved by the House of Bishops; the approval of a majority of the diocesan synods is also necessary (SGM sched. 2, arts. 7, 8). A two-thirds majority in each house of SYNOD is required before a canon dealing with DOCTRINE or worship may be submitted for royal licence and assent (C of E (W and D)M s. 3). See **Eucharist**.

SACRED IMAGES (L *sacrae imagines*)

   RC. Statues, icons, paintings, etc. of the Blessed Virgin and of the SAINTS. The veneration of the Blessed Virgin Mary and of the saints is encouraged 'in order to foster the sanctification of the people of God' (c 1186; see also *SC* 103–4, *LG* 52–69). Sacred images may be exposed in CHURCHES, with a *proviso* that they are 'displayed in moderate numbers, and in suitable fashion' (c 1188).

C of E. Since the introduction of sacred images into a church would involve an alteration to the content of a consecrated building, they would require a FACULTY. The diocesan CHANCELLOR would have to consider their aesthetic character, whether or not such objects have been considered illegal by previous case law, and whether or not they are likely to give rise to superstitious reverence. In *Re St Mary's, Tyne Dock (no. 1)* [1954] 2 All ER 339 at 346, Hylton-Foster Ch ordered the removal of a statue of the Blessed Virgin since he felt that its presence was a subject of dissension in the PARISH.

SACRILEGE (L *sacrilegium*)

RC. The wilful use of sacred things for a purpose which destroys their sacredness. A person, for example, who throws away the consecrated species or who takes them or retains them for a purpose which is sacrilegious incurs an automatic EXCOMMUNICATION. If a CLERIC, he can be punished with dismissal from the clerical state (c 1367). Sacrilege is a more serious offence than PROFANATION. See **Blasphemy**; *Latae Sententiae*.

C of E. A violation or an abuse of a sacred person, sacred place or sacred thing.

SAINT (L *sanctus*)

RC. A departed servant of God who lived a life of holiness while on earth. **Cult of saints**: the Church 'promotes the true and authentic cult' of the Blessed Virgin Mary and of the saints (c 1186). The veneration of the saints is encouraged for the edification of the people of God; God's people are also supported by the intercession of the saints (*LG* 52–69). **Canonization of saints**: the solemn proclamation of the heroic virtue of those whose lives were faithful to God's grace: see John Paul II: apostolic constitution *Divinus Perfectionis Magister* (1983). See **Appendix I**.

C of E. Saints are commemorated with praise and thanksgiving on RED-LETTER and BLACK-LETTER DAYS in the Church's calendar. The Church rejects the practice of 'the cult' of saints, i.e. the veneration and intercession of saints. See **Black-Letter Days**; **Feast Day**; **Feast of Obligation**; **Red-Letter Days**.

SCHISM (L *schisma*, Gk σχίσμα, split)

RC. Generally speaking, a breach in Church unity or ecclesial communion. In the strict canonical sense, a breach of communion with the pope, i.e. a refusal to submit to the pope or a refusal of communion with members of the Church subject to him (c 751). See **Apostasy**; **Heresy**.

C of E. Since the unity of the Church is impaired and the witness to Christ's Gospel is grievously hindered by schism, clergy and people have a duty to avoid occasions of strife and also to seek in love and charity to heal divisions (canon A8). The Church does not define schism.

AC. Schism, however, is defined in the laws of some Churches of the ANGLICAN COMMUNION. For example, in Southern Africa and West Africa it is defined as 'acceptance or promotion of membership in a religious body not in communion' with the Church (Southern Africa, can 37. 1(d)–(f); West Africa Const. art. XXII, 6(d)–(f)).

SECULAR INSTITUTES: see **Institutes of Consecrated Life**.

SEDE VACANTE (L, the see being vacant)

RC. **Episcopal See**: as soon as an episcopal SEE becomes vacant the coadjutor BISHOP becomes the bishop of the DIOCESE. An auxiliary bishop retains such powers and faculties as he possessed as VICAR general or episcopal vicar, upon the vacancy (c 409 §§1, 2). An episcopal See becomes vacant upon the death of a diocesan bishop, or upon his resignation, or upon transferral or deprivation of office (c 416). A diocesan ADMINISTRATOR must be elected by the College of Consultors to govern the diocese in the interim period, within eight days of receiving notice that the See is vacant (c 421 §1). **Apostolic See**: during a vacancy the government of the Church is in the hands of the College of Cardinals 'solely for the dispatch of ordinary business and of matters which cannot be postponed . . . , and for the preparation of everything necessary for the election of the new Pope' (*UDG* ch. 1(2)). All heads of the DICASTERIES of the Roman *CURIA* cease to exercise their office, with the exception of the CARDINAL CAMERLENGO and the Major Penitentiary (*PB* art. 6; *UDG* ch. 3(14)). The Cardinal Vicar General of the diocese of Rome, the Cardinal Archpriest of the Vatican Basilica and the Vicar General for the Vatican City also continue in office (*UDG* ch. 3(14); *VP* 2). **Vacant Parish**: when a PARISH becomes vacant or a pastor is unable to exercise his pastoral office the diocesan bishop is to appoint a parochial administrator as soon as possible (c 539). Until a parochial administrator is appointed a parochial vicar is to assume governance of the parish (c 541 §1).

C of E. During such vacancy the ARCHBISHOP acts as guardian of the spiritualities of the diocese and appoints a COMMISSARY to act for him.

SEE

RC. The seat of a BISHOP. The episcopal See is occupied by the bishop of the DIOCESE.

C of E. A bishopric. See **Bishop**.

SENTENCE (L *sententia*)

RC. A judgement or a legal pronouncement. **Definitive sentence**: a sentence upon a matter which is the 'principal case' (c 1607). **Interlocutory sentence**: a judgement which decides a matter which is incidental in the case (c 1607, 1587–91). **Declaratory sentence**: an automatic PENALTY (*LATAE SENTENTIAE*) which is incurred by the very commission of an offence. **Condemnatory sentence**: a penalty which is inflicted by a sentence which is binding only after it is imposed (*FERENDAE SENTENTIAE*). See **Censure**.

SEQUESTRATION (L *sequestratio*)

RC. The entrusting of a person or an object under dispute to a third party. **Right of sequestration**: a person who has shown a right to something which another retains, and who has shown there is a threat of damage if that object is not handed over for safe keeping, has a right to obtain its sequestration by a judge (c 1496 §1). See **Inhibition**.

C of E. The CHURCHWARDENS and RURAL DEAN become the sequestrators of a BENEFICE if it becomes vacant otherwise than through the resignation of the INCUMBENT (C of E (MP)M s. 1(1)).

SERMON: see **Homily**.

SIMONY (L *simonia*)

RC. A PRESBYTER is forbidden to request payment for the administration of a SACRAMENT over and above the offerings established by a competent authority (c 848). If a person 'traffics for profit' in MASS OFFERINGS he is to be punished with a CENSURE or other just PENALTY (c 1385). Simoniacal conferral of an ecclesiastical office or resignation from such an office submitted because of simony is invalid in law (cc 149 §3; 188). Simoniacal conferral or reception of a sacrament is punishable with an INTERDICT or a SUSPENSION (c 1380).

C of E. The buying or selling, in particular, of holy ORDERS or of ecclesiastical BENEFICES (SA).

SOCIETIES OF APOSTOLIC LIFE (L *societates apostolicae vitae*)

RC. Societies whose members live a common fraternal life and 'pursue the apostolic purpose proper to each society', but do not take religious

Vows – at least, not public vows. For example, the Oratorians established by St Philip Neri in the sixteenth century. See **Institutes of Consecrated Life**.

SOLICITATION (L *solicitatio*)

RC. **Solicitation of a penitent**: an invitation by a PRESBYTER to a penitent to commit a serious sin against the sixth commandment of the Decalogue, made in the context or under the pretext of CONFESSION. A PRIEST who acts in this way is punishable with SUSPENSION, prohibition, deprivation or even with dismissal from the clerical state (c 1387). If a confessor is falsely accused of solicitation by a person before an ecclesiastical superior that person incurs an automatic INTERDICT and, if a CLERIC, also a suspension (c 1390 §1). If a person confesses to a false denunciation he or she can only be absolved after formally retracting the denunciation and declaring a willingness to make reparation for the harm done (c 982). **Solicitation of funds**: Persons (apart from religious mendicants) may start fund-raising for pious or ecclesiastical institutions or purposes only with the written permission of their own ORDINARY or the ordinary of the place where the funds will be raised (c 1265 §1).

SOURCES

RC. **Historical sources**: these include canonical collections, pontificals, texts and DECRETALS. **Sources of law or custom**: these are created by the pope or a council. **Official legislative texts and customs** which are in force: these include *CIC* and the general DECREES of episcopal conferences. **Suppletive sources**: principles adopted by the Church for supplying what is wanting in its own legislation, i.e. where a law or CUSTOM is lacking in a non-penal matter (c 19).

C of E. Statute law and principles of COMMON LAW developed by the courts are important sources of law. So also are MEASURES, CANONS, custom, PRECEDENT and RUBRICS. The views of text-writers are of lesser importance than in the Catholic Church. See **Act**.

SPONSOR

RC. One who, along with the parents, presents an infant at BAPTISM and helps him or her to live a Christian life; also, one who assists an adult in Christian initiation. Only one male or one female sponsor or one of each sex are allowed (cc 872–4, 774, 851). The sponsor for one to be confirmed is to see that the confirmed person acts as a true witness to Christ and is faithful in fulfilling the obligations connected with the SACRAMENT (c 892). The term 'sponsor' is used for 'godparent' (*patrinus*) in translating *CIC*.

C of E. Three godparents are required for infant baptism; two are to be of the same sex as the child and at least one of the opposite sex (canon B23(1)). They are to 'faithfully fulfil their responsibilities both by the care for the child and in their example of their own godly living' (canon B23(2)). A candidate for adult baptism may choose either two or three sponsors (canon B23(3)). A godparent or sponsor must be both baptized and confirmed, although the minister is empowered to dispense with the latter requirement where necessary (canon B23(4)).

STARE DECISIS (L, keep to what has been decided)

C of E. A rule belonging to the doctrine of PRECEDENT whereby the decisions of past cases must be followed. See ***Ratio Decidendi***.

STAUROPEGIACUS (Gk σταυροπήγιον, the fixing of a cross on the spot where a church is to be built).

EC. A monastery which comes under the direct authority of the patriarch so that he alone enjoys the rights and obligations of an eparchial BISHOP towards it, its members and those who stay there (*CCEO* c 486 §2).

STIPEND (L *stipendium*, income)

C of E. The financial remuneration of CLERICS for their services. Stipends are raised from the QUOTA levied upon PARISHES. **Non-stipendary** (or **self-supporting**) **ministers**: clerics who are engaged in secular employment and who are engaged in ministry on a part-time basis.

SUBREPTION (L *subreptio*)

RC. The 'withholding of the truth' in a petition (c 63 §1). Subreption makes a RESCRIPT invalid when it affects the conditions laid down by law or contained in NORMS, general guidelines, etc. For example, all irregularities and IMPEDIMENTS must be mentioned in a petition for a DISPENSATION (c 1049 §1). If a favour is granted *MOTU PROPRIO* then a rescript is not invalidated by subreption (c 63 §1). Subreption may be punishable with an ecclesiastical PENALTY (c 1391). See **Obreption**.

SUBSIDIARITY (L *subsidiarietas*)

RC. A principle which is prominent in the social teaching of the Church. According to the principle all social bodies exist for the sake of the person. Social bodies, therefore, should not take over the role of individuals or small societies. Moreover, what individuals are unable to do, society should do for them – see, for example, Pius XI: *Quadragesimo Anno* (1931). It is a principle which is applied to civil society, and in the Church with respect to its hierarchical order. Under

Paul VI it was accepted as a principle to guide the revision of CANON LAW. The principle is applied in the Church in order to strengthen the bond between those who exercise authority and those who are subject to authority.

SUI COMPOS (L)

RC. Having the use of reason. A minor is presumed to have the use of reason at seven years of age (c 97(2)). In terms of ECCLESIASTICAL LAW a seven-year-old is ready to address himself or herself to religious responsibility and observance (c 11). Any person lacking the use of reason is held to be incompetent (*non sui compos*) and is equated with infants (c 99).

SUI IURIS (L, of its own right)

RC. Autonomous. **Religious houses** *sui iuris*: a religious house such as an abbey which is autonomous with regard to its internal government, having its own moderator (cc 613, 615). See **Abbot**. **Churches** *sui iuris*: a Church united by a hierarchy according to the NORM of law which the Supreme Authority of the Church recognizes as autonomous with regard to government and discipline (*CCEO* c 27); examples include the Latin, the Ukrainian and the Melkite Churches. Churches of the Latin and Western rites are *sui iuris* in accordance with the norm of law. Eastern Churches *sui iuris* include PATRIARCHAL CHURCHES (*CCEO* c 55), major archiepiscopal Churches (*CCEO* c 151), METROPOLITAN CHURCHES (*CCEO* c 155) and certain other Churches which have acquired autonomy (*CCEO* c 174).

SUPER (MATRIMONIO) RATO (L, on a ratified marriage)

RC. A DISPENSATION is *super rato* when a MARRIAGE is dispensed from when it has been ratified but not consummated. The parties (or one party) have the right to seek dispensation from such a marriage. Once the case has undergone instruction at a local level, the petition and ACTS are sent to the APOSTOLIC SEE. The pope may then grant dispensation upon the recommendation of the Congregation for Divine Worship and the Discipline of the Sacraments. The marriage is thereby dissolved (C Sac lit. circ. *De Processu Super Matrimonio Rato et non Consummato* (1986): *ME* 112 (1981) 423–8. See **Indissolubility**.

SURROGATE (L *subrogo*)

C of E. A deputy who grants MARRIAGE licences on behalf of the diocesan VICAR general (who is also the CHANCELLOR of the DIOCESE). The surrogate is a CLERIC appointed by a judge upon the BISHOP'S recommendation. His appointment is testified by a commission under seal which includes an OATH of office: the surrogate must swear 'faithfully to execute his office according to law, to the best of his knowledge' (*MA* 1949 s. 16(4)).

SUSPENSION (L *suspensio*)

RC. A medicinal PENALTY or CENSURE incurred only by CLERICS which is less prohibitive than EXCOMMUNICATION or INTERDICT. A cleric can be suspended from total or partial exercise of his ORDERS (*suspensio ab ordinibus*), from total or partial power of governance (*suspensio a jurisdictione*) or from all or some functions of office (*suspensio ab officio*) (c 1333). Only the law (not a PRECEPT) can establish an automatic suspension which incurs the above penalties (c 1334 §2).

C of E. A censure imposed upon a cleric who has committed an offence. It involves disqualification for a specified time from the exercise of clerical duties or from residing in the parsonage house (EJM ss. 71, 72). **Suspension of a living**: where there is a vacancy the BISHOP may suspend the living for up to five years (PM s. 67).

SYNAXIS (L, Gk σύναξις)

RC. An assembly, a banquet. In the Eucharistic banquet God's people are called together to participate in their own way according to the diversity of ORDERS and liturgical roles (c 899 §2).

SYNCELLI (Gk σύγκελλος, cell sharer)

EC. PRESBYTERS (usually celibate) who are appointed by the eparchial BISHOP to conduct certain types of business in a determined section of the EPARCHY. They have the same authority as the PROTOSYNCELLUS (*CCEO* cc 246; 247 §§1, 2. Their equivalent in *CIC* are episcopal VICARS.

SYNCELLUS (Gk σύγκελλος, cell sharer)

EC. A word mostly used in the Eastern Church to describe a CLERIC who resided with a BISHOP (e.g. his CHAPLAIN) so that he could attest to the bishop's purity of life. The word came to describe a clerical dignitary who acted as counsellor to a PRELATE and who later succeeded him. See **Protosyncellus**; **Syncelli**.

SYNOD (L *synodus*, Gk σύνοδος)

RC. Synod of bishops: a group of BISHOPS chosen from different parts of the world who represent the whole Catholic EPISCOPATE. The functions of the synod are to draw members of the COLLEGE OF BISHOPS closer to each other, to advise the pope on Church governance and to consider the role of the Church in the world (c 342). The synod's role is consultative rather than deliberative; it acts deliberatively when empowered to do so by the pope (c 343). **Diocesan synod**: a gathering of elected members of the clergy and LAITY in the DIOCESE under the presidency of the bishop. The bishop alone can legislate at the synod; other members have only a consultative vote (c 466; see cc 460–8). See **Diocese**.

C of E. **Diocesan synod**: this comprises a House of Bishops, a House of Clergy and a House of Laity: membership is governed by CRR r. 30. Its functions include the implementation of Church matters in the diocese and advising the bishop when requested (SGM ss. 4(2)(a), (b)). **Deanery synod**: this comprises a House of Clergy and a House of Laity: membership is governed by CRR r. 24. Its functions include the implementation of Church matters in the deanery. **Area synod**: this is constituted when a diocese is divided into episcopal areas under a suffragan bishop or bishops (DM s. 17). See also **General Synod**.

T

TABERNACLE (L *tabernaculum*)

RC. A decorated receptacle for the blessed SACRAMENT, which is usually placed behind the main ALTAR or in the side chapel of a church. It is covered with a veil and has a lighted lamp beside it (cc 938, 940; SCRit instruction *Eucharisticum Mysterium* (1967)).

C of E. RESERVATION OF THE EUCHARIST in a tabernacle has been held to be illegal (*Re Lapford (Devon) Parish Church* [1954] 3 All ER 484). The sacrament may be reserved in an AUMBRY or hanging pyx (*Re St Nicholas, Plumstead* [1961] 1 WLR 916).

TAX (L *subsidium*, aid)

RC. A means of support for a DIOCESE and its programmes. The diocesan BISHOP may impose a tax on public JURIDICAL PERSONS under his authority in so far as is necessary for the needs of the diocese. The tax must be moderate and proportionate to their income although in situations of grave necessity an 'extraordinary' tax may be levied. Before levying a tax the BISHOP must consult the financial council and the PRESBYTERAL COUNCIL (c 1263). See **Quota**.

TERNUS (L, three each)

RC. The system for determining the composition of various panels of judges of the Roman ROTA. Rotal judges serve in panels of three, five, seven, or as a panel of the whole body.

TITLE (L *titulus*)

C of E. An ecclesiastical preferment with guarantee of maintenance which awaits a person who is to be admitted to holy ORDERS, where that person may attend the cure of souls and execute his or her ministry. The diocesan BISHOP cannot ordain a person into holy orders unless he or she has been provided with an ecclesiastical office (canon C5(1)). See **Order**.

TRANSACTIO (L, completion)

RC. A settlement or reconciliation between parties over a private matter with a view to avoiding judicial contention (cc 1713–16).

Transfer (L *transfero*)

RC. An act of a competent authority by which an office-holder changes office (cc 190, 191). The movement of a member of an Institute of Consecrated Life or a Society of Apostolic Life from one institute or society to another (cc 684, 730, 744).

U

UNIVERSAL LAW (L *ius universum*)

RC. A law which is binding upon everyone for whom it was made, throughout the entire Church (c 12 §§1, 2). See **Particular Law**.

V

VACATIO LEGIS (L, exemption from the law)

RC. A given length of time during which the force of a law is temporarily suspended. This happens in order to give members of the Church time to become acquainted with the law – e.g. for the laws of the APOSTOLIC SEE a respite of three months is granted from the date of their publication in the *Acta Apostolicae Sedis*. See *Acta*.

VAGUS (L, wandering)

RC. A CLERIC who is not incardinated; an itinerant cleric. See *Acephalus*; **Incardination**. A transient person, one who has neither DOMICILE nor quasi-domicile in any place (c 100). See *Peregrinus*.

VENERABLE (L *venerabilis*)

RC. A title bestowed after death upon a faithful Catholic as a stage in the process of BEATIFICATION; e.g. The Venerable John Henry Newman (1801–90). An official DECREE is published proclaiming the person's exercise of heroic virtues, which might include martyrdom. The title is used in a general sense to refer to a person who has lived a life of marked holiness (e.g. The Venerable Bede). See **Canonization**; **Promoter of the Faith**; **Appendix I**.

C of E. The style of an ARCHDEACON.

VENIAL SIN (L *peccatum veniabile*)

RC. A sin that is not grave. The confession of venial sins is recommended although not obligatory (c 988 §2). See **Grave Sin**.

VETITUM (L)

RC. A prohibition attached to a judgement or DECREE of a tribunal in a NULLITY of MARRIAGE appeal case (c 1684 §1). Such a prohibition prevents the contracting of a new marriage. A temporary prohibition may be imposed by the local ORDINARY 'in a specific case' but 'only for a grave reason' (c 1077 §1) – for example, if there were strong grounds for believing that a marriage would be invalid. Prohibitions are imposed in cases of simulation, absolute impotence, mental illness, etc. They may be temporary or permanent. See **Impediment**.

V*IATICUM* (L, provision for a journey)

RC. The bringing of Eucharistic Communion to the sick and to those in danger of death. A minister of Holy Communion has a right and duty to do so (cc 911, 921, 922).

C of E. A priest is to administer Holy Communion to a person who is sick or in danger of death if that person so desires (canon B37(2)). See **Eucharist**.

V*ICAR* (L *vicarius*)

RC. **Vicar of Christ**: a title of the pope (c 331). **Vicar general**: a priest whom the diocesan B*ISHOP* appoints to help him with the governance of his D*IOCESE* (c 475). **Episcopal vicar**: a P*RIEST* whom the diocesan bishop can appoint to help him govern his diocese (c 476). Both offices carry O*RDINARY*, executive power. **Judicial vicar**: a priest whom the diocesan bishop appoints and who has ordinary power to judge cases in his tribunal (c 1420). **Parochial vicar**: a priest who is assigned to help a pastor in his care of a P*ARISH* (c 545). **Vicar forane**: a priest appointed by a diocesan bishop to have pastoral care of a group of parishes or a deanery (c 553–5). **Apostolic vicar**: a priest who has pastoral care of a non-diocesan area (c 371). See **Official**.

C of E. The holder of a B*ENEFICE* who has a F*REEHOLD* interest in its emoluments. He or she has the cure of souls within the parish. Historically, the vicar was the deputy of the R*ECTOR*. **Vicar general**: a C*OMMISSARY* through whom an A*RCHBISHOP* or a diocesan bishop exercises J*URISDICTION* (canon C18(3)). It is the provincial vicar general who grants M*ARRIAGE* licences on behalf of the metropolitan. It is the diocesan vicar general who acts likewise on behalf of the ordinary. In practice, deputies or S*URROGATES* are appointed to issue such licences in a diocese.

V*ISITATION* (L *visitatio*)

RC. An inspection carried out by (*a*) the metropolitan B*ISHOP* within a suffragan D*IOCESE* where the suffragan has neglected it, with the approval of the A*POSTOLIC* S*EE* (c 436 (2)); (*b*) by the V*ICAR* forane, who is obliged to visit the P*ARISHES* of the district, when required, in accordance with regulations made by the diocesan bishop (c 555 §4); (*c*) by the diocesan bishop, who is obliged to visit his diocese every year, wholly or in part, so that the diocese as a whole is visited at least every five years (c 396 §1). See *Ad limina* **visit**; **Archbishop**; **Bishop**.

C of E. A quasi-judicial function carried out annually by every A*RCHDEACON* in his archdeaconry on behalf of the diocesan bishop, save when the bishop does so himself (canon C22(5)); the archdeacon exercises ORDINARY JURISDICTION when he holds his visitation (canon C22(2)). ARCHBISHOPS, bishops and archdeacons have a right to hold visitations in PROVINCES, dioceses and archdeaconries respectively for the good government and edification of the church (canon G5). In holding a visitation the bishop has an opportunity to get to know ministers and CHURCHWARDENS better. The minister and churchwardens are obliged to reply to the archdeacon's articles of inquiry into the state of the parish when he summons his visitation (canon G6). At a visitation churchwardens are admitted to office and their presentments (i.e. their presentation of what in the parish is irregular or amiss) are received. See **Ordinary**.

Vow (L *votum*)

RC. 'A deliberate and free promise' which is made to God concerning a better good (c 1191 §1). **Public vow**: a vow received 'in the name of the Church' by a lawful superior. An individual's vow otherwise remains *private* (c 1192 §1). **Solemn vow**: a vow which is recognized by the Church as *solemn*. If they are not recognized as such by the Church, they remain *simple* vows (c 1192 §2). **Personal, real** or **mixed vow**: *personal* vows are promises to do something, e.g. to assist at daily Mass; *real* vows are promises of something, e.g. to make a special donation to the poor; *mixed* vows are vows which are both *personal* and *real* in nature (c 1192 §3).

Appendix I

Causes for the Canonization of Saints

Apostolic Constitution Divinus Perfectionis Magister *(25 January 1983)*

RC. This apostolic constitution revises the way in which the causes of SAINTS are drawn up, in order to meet the needs of both scholars and BISHOPS. It also brings the bishops into closer association with the APOSTOLIC SEE in the processing of causes of saints.

Chapter I. Diocesan bishops (and others of equal legal standing) have the right 'to investigate the life, virtues or martyrdom, and the reputation for holiness or martyrdom, the alleged miracles, as well as, if the case so warrants, the age-long public cult to the Servant of God whose CANONIZATION is being sought' (art. 1). A diocesan bishop according to the procedure published by the Sacred Congregation for Causes of Saints must act as follows: (i) he must seek accurate information about the servant of God from the Postulator of the Cause and be instructed by him upon the reason in favour of the Cause of Canonization; (ii) he must make sure that any published writings by the Servant of God are examined by theologian censors; (iii) provided that these published writings are not in any way contrary to faith or morals the diocesan bishop must make sure that any unpublished writings and documents are 'diligently' examined and reported upon by persons qualified to do so; (iv) if in his judgement the matter can proceed further he must see to it that witnesses and others produced by the postulator are examined; (v) the investigation of alleged miracles and the investigation regarding virtues or martyrdom must be undertaken separately; (vi) when all investigations have been carried out the Sacred congregation is to receive a certified copy of all the acts in duplicate and a copy of the books of the Servant of God which the theologian censors have examined (along with their judgements); (vii) the diocesan bishop is to append a declaration concerning the observance of the DECREES of Pope Urban VIII concerning lack of public cult.

Chapter II. A CARDINAL prefect (and a secretary) presides over the Congregation for Causes of Saints. The congregation is to assist the bishops 'by instructions and by in-depth study of the causes, and, finally, by giving its opinions' (art. 3). A College of Reporters presided over by a reporter general study the causes within the congregation. A

PROMOTER OF THE FAITH (a PRELATE theologian) is chosen from within the congregation in order to: (i) preside over the assembly of theologians (wherein he has a vote); (ii) report on the assembly itself; (iii) be present at the session of the cardinals and bishops in an expert capacity only. Consultors are present in an expert capacity when the causes are examined. Medical experts are also included with the congregation in order to examine health cures which are considered to be miraculous. Cardinals and bishops give a report of their decisions to the Supreme Pontiff who alone has the right to decide upon a Servant of God's canonization.

C of E. The GENERAL SYNOD of the Church has the power 'to approve Holy Days which may be observed locally', provided that directions laid down by 'the Convocation of the province' are followed (canons B6(5), B2)). The table of 'Lesser Festivals and Commemorations' in the ASB includes, for example, 'George Herbert, Priest, Pastor, Poet, 1633' on January 27 and 'William Wilberforce, a Social Reformer, 1833' on July 29. The Church prefers not to refer to such persons as 'saints'. However, on the day of their commemoration, the collect and readings 'of any saint' may be used (ASB p. 18). See **Feast Day**.

Appendix II

Military Ordinariates

Apostolic Constitution Spirituali Militum Curae *(24 April 1986)*

RC. These are 'special ecclesiastical districts governed by proper statutes issued by the Apostolic See' (*SMC* I §1). When *CIC* was promulgated the NORMS issued by the Sacred Consistorial Congregations in 1951 for the spiritual care of military people were still in force (see instruction *Sollemne Semper*, 23 April 1951; *CIC* c 569).

According to the revised norms a military ordinariate is under the charge of an ORDINARY who is usually a BISHOP with the rights and obligations of a diocesan bishop (*SMC* II §1). The ordinary is a member of the Conference of Bishops of the country in which he is situated (*SMC* III). His JURISDICTION is in addition to the diocesan bishop's jurisdiction over the PARTICULAR CHURCH in which the ordinariate is situated (*SCM* IV 3°). When the military ordinary and military chaplains are away the diocesan bishop and PARISH PRIEST exercise jurisdiction (*SMC* V). The military ordinary, with the approval of the HOLY SEE, can erect a seminary to prepare candidates for holy ORDERS in the ordinariate (*SMC* VI §3). He is subject to the Congregation for Bishops or the Congregation for the Evangelization of Peoples (*SMC* XI); he must make an AD LIMINA VISIT in accordance with the law (*CIC* cc 399; 400 §1–2). Those subject to the jurisdiction of the military ordinariate include: '1°, the faithful who are military persons, as well as those who are at the service of the armed forces provided they are bound to this by civil laws; 2°, all the members of their families, wives and children, even those who though independent, live in the same house, as well as relatives and servants who also live with them in the same house; 3°, those who attend military training schools or who live or work in military hospitals, hospices for the elderly, or similar institutions; 4°, all the faithful, both men and women, whether or not they are members of a religious institute, who carry out in a permanent way a task committed to them by the Military Ordinary, or with his consent' (*SMC* X).

Judicial cases regarding the faithful of the Military Ordinariate can be heard in the first INSTANCE by the tribunal of the DIOCESE in which the *Curia* of the Military Ordinariate lies; this situation arises when the Ordinariate does not have its own tribunal (*SMC* XIV).

C of E. CHAPLAINS to the armed forces are licensed to officiate by the Archbishop of Canterbury and are under his jurisdiction which is exercised by the Bishop to the Forces who is a suffragan bishop in the PROVINCE of Canterbury. They are supervised by Chief Chaplains to the armed forces who are styled ARCHDEACONS.

Appendix III

Reorganization of the Roman Curia

Apostolic Constitution Pastor Bonus *(28 June 1988)*

RC. This apostolic constitution on the reorganization of the Roman CURIA produces change in six main areas. (i) The *Curia* itself. *Pastor Bonus* speaks of the pope's 'supreme pastoral office' (art. 1) and not of his 'supreme, full and immediate power' (*CD* 9; also c 360). Greater emphasis is laid upon the *Curia* as serving the pope alone and not the COLLEGE OF BISHOPS (art. 1). (ii) Its Organization. Firstly, the DICASTERIES (the main bodies of the *Curia*) have been reorganized and simplified. In this document the Council for the Public Affairs of the Church is amalgamated into the Secretariat of State, the number of congregations is reduced from ten to nine, while the three secretariats and the twenty-eight councils and commissions are reorganized into twelve pontifical councils. The seven offices of the *Curia* are now reduced to three. Secondly, the Congregation on the Doctrine of the Faith has been given higher juridical status than other dicasteries. It now has a right of prior judgement over all documents about to be issued by them 'in so far as they touch on the doctrine of faith or morals' (art. 54). (iii) Competence. A group of CARDINALS who meet regularly to deal with the finances of the APOSTOLIC SEE have been formed into a Council of Cardinals for the Study of Organizational and Economic Problems of the Apostolic See. This council comprises fifteen cardinals who are diocesan BISHOPS. They are to serve for a term of five years and are to meet usually twice a year. Their competence now covers organizational as well as economic matters (arts. 24, 25). Under *Pastor Bonus* all serious criminal cases in the celebration of the SACRAMENTS are to be referred to the Congregation of the Faith and not to the Congregation of the Sacraments (art. 52). (iv) The *Curia*'s relationship with PARTICULAR CHURCHES and their groupings. The advice of particular Churches should now be sought in preparing major documents of a general nature (art. 26 §1). This is to be done through bishops' conferences in the Latin Church, and episcopal SYNODS in the EASTERN CATHOLIC CHURCHES. Particular Churches are to be consulted by the Secretariat of State in developing Church–state relations (art. 46); they are to be given assistance in their teaching function by the Congregation for the Doctrine of the Faith (art. 50); also by the Pontifical Council for the Interpretation of Legislative Texts in deciding if proposed laws are in keeping with Universal Law (art. 158); their Decrees and their translations of liturgical texts are subject to review (arts. 157; 64 §3); respect is to be shown towards their rights regarding vocations and seminaries (art. 93). (v) Personnel. This document establishes a Central Labour Office to address the staffing of the *Curia* (art. 36). (vi) *Ad limina* visits. *Pastor Bonus* emphazises the importance of these visits as a sign of the communion which binds the pope and bishops. They include a pilgrimage to the tombs of the apostles Peter and Paul, a personal visit to the pope, and visits to the dicasteries of the Roman *Curia*. See *Ad Limina* **Visit**.

Dictionaries and Reference Books

CROSS, F. L., and LIVINGSTONE, E. A., *Oxford Dictionary of the Christian Church* (3rd edn., Oxford, 1997)

GLARE, P. G. W., ed., *Oxford Latin Dictionary* (Oxford, 1982)

LEWIS, C. T., and SHORT, C. S., *A Latin Dictionary* (Oxford, 1955)

SIMPSON, J. A., and WEINER, E. S. C., eds., *Oxford English Dictionary* (2nd edn., Oxford, 1989)

SOPHOCLES, E. A., *A Greek Lexicon of the Roman and Byzantine Periods* (Oxford, 1914)

STELTEN, L. F., *Dictionary of Ecclesiastical Latin* (3rd printing, Massachusetts, 1997)

WALKER, D. M., *Oxford Companion to Law* (Oxford, 1980)

WERCKMEISTER, J., *Petit Dictionnaire de Droit Canonique* (Paris, 1993)

Textbooks, Booklets
and Commentaries

BRAY, G., ed., *The Anglican Canons 1529–1947* (Woodbridge, Suffolk, 1998)

BRIDEN, T., and HANSON, B., eds, *Moore's Introduction to English Canon Law* (3rd edn., London, 1992)

BURN, R., *Ecclesiastical Law* (9th edn., London, 1842)

BURSELL, R. D. H., *Liturgy, Order and the Law* (Oxford, 1996)

The Canon Law Society of Great Britain and Ireland, *The Canon Law. Letter and Spirit* (London, 1995)

The Canons of the Church of England. Canons Ecclesiastical promulged by the Convocations of Canterbury and York in 1964 and 1969, and by the General Synod of the Church of England from 1970 (5th edn., London, 1993)

CAPARROS, E., THÉRIAULT, M., and THORN, J., eds., *The Code of Canon Law, Annotated* (Montreal, 1993)

Codex Canonum Ecclesiarum Orientalium (Vatican Press, 1990: the Eastern Catholic code of canon law)

Codex Iuris Canonici (Vatican Press, 1983: the Roman Catholic code of canon law)

CORIDEN, J. A., *An Introduction to the Canon Law* (London, 1991)

——, GREEN, T. J., and HEINTSCHEL, D. E., eds., *The Code of Canon Law* (New York, 1983)

DEPUIS, J., ed., *Neuner and Depuis: The Christian Faith in the Doctrinal Documents of the Catholic Church* (6th rev. and enlarged edn., New York, 1996)

A Directory of the Religious Life (4th edn., London, 1990)

DOE, N., *The Legal Framework of the Church of England* (Oxford, 1996)

——, *Canon Law in the Anglican Communion* (Oxford, 1998)

FLANNERY, A., ed., *Vatican II: The Conciliar and Post Conciliar Documents* (rev. edn., New York, 1992)

GALLEN, J. E., *Canon Law for Religious* (New York, 1983)

HALSBURY, H. S. G., *Laws of England*, vol. 14: *Ecclesiastical Law* (4th edn., London, 1975)

HILL, M., *Ecclesiastical Law* (London, 1995)

HITE, J., and WARD, D. J., eds., *Readings, Cases, Materials in Canon Law: A Text for Ministerial Students* (rev. edn., Minnesota, 1990).

HUELS, J. M., *The Pastoral Companion: A Canon Law Handbook for Catholic Ministry* (2nd edn., Quincy, 1995).

LEEDER, L., *Ecclesiastical Law Handbook* (London, 1997)

MCAREAVEY, J., *The Canon Law of Marriage and the Family* (Dublin, 1997)

MILLER, J. M., ed., *The Encyclicals of John Paul II* (Indiana, 1996)

MORRISEY, F. G., *Papal and Curial Pronouncements: their Canonical Significance in Light of the Code of Canon Law* (2nd edn., Ottawa, 1995)

NEWSOM, G. H., *Faculty Jurisdiction of the Church of England* (2nd edn., London, 1993)

POSPISHIL, V. J., 'The Code of Canons of the Eastern Churches', in *Eastern Catholic Church Law* (2nd rev. and augm. edn., New York, 1996)

THOMAS, E. L. ed., *Baker's Law Relating to Burials* (6th edn., London, 1901)

Articles

ENGELHARDT, H., 'The Lawyer's Contribution to the Progress of Christian Unity', *Ecumenical Review* 21 (1969), 7

ÖRSY, L., 'Towards a Theological Conception of Canon Law', in Hite and Ward, *Readings*, 10

PROVOST, J. H., 'Pastor Bonus: Reflections on the Reorganisation of the Roman Curia' *Jurist* 48 (1988), 499–534

WATKIN, T. G., 'Vestiges of Establishment: The Ecclesiastical and Canon Law of the Church in Wales', *Ecclesiastical Law Journal* 2 (1990)